To Mitesh

hope that this is
both useful and fun!
i look forward to
trying some !!
Happy Christmas 2006

Flavorful

India

from
Richard

The Hippocrene Cookbook Library

Afghan Food & Cookery
African Cooking, Best of Regional
Albanian Cooking, Best of
Alps, Cuisines of The
Aprovecho: A Mexican-American Border Cookbook
Argentina Cooks!, Exp. Ed.
Austrian Cuisine, Best of, Exp. Ed.
Belgian Cookbook, A
Bolivian Kitchen, My Mother's
Brazilian Cookery, The Art of
Bulgarian Cooking, Traditional
Burma, Flavors of,
Cajun Women, Cooking With
Calabria, Cucina di
Caucasus Mountains, Cuisines of the
Chile, Tasting
Colombian, Secrets of Cooking
Croatian Cooking, Best of, Exp. Ed.
Czech Cooking, Best of, Exp. Ed.
Danube, All Along The, Exp. Ed.
Dutch Cooking, Art of, Exp. Ed.
Egyptian Cooking
Eritrea, Taste of
Filipino Food, Fine
Finnish Cooking, Best of
French Caribbean Cuisine
French Fashion, Cooking in the
    (Bilingual)
Germany, Spoonfuls of
Greek Cuisine, The Best of, Exp. Ed.
Gypsy Feast
Haiti, Taste of
Havana Cookbook, Old (Bilingual)
Hungarian Cookbook
Hungarian Cooking, Art of, Rev. Ed.
Icelandic Food & Cookery
India, Flavorful
Indian Spice Kitchen
International Dictionary of Gastronomy
Irish-Style, Feasting Galore
Italian Cuisine, Treasury of (Bilingual)
Japanese Home Cooking
Korean Cuisine, Best of
Laotian Cooking, Simple

Latvia, Taste of
Lithuanian Cooking, Art of
Macau, Taste of
Mayan Cooking
Middle Eastern Kitchen, The
Mongolian Cooking, Imperial
New Hampshire: From Farm to Kitchen
Norway, Tastes and Tales of
Persian Cooking, Art of
Poland's Gourmet Cuisine
Polish Cooking, Best of, Exp. Ed.
Polish Country Kitchen Cookbook
Polish Cuisine, Treasury of (Bilingual)
Polish Heritage Cookery, Ill. Ed.
Polish Traditions, Old
Portuguese Encounters, Cuisines of
Pyrenees, Tastes of
Quebec, Taste of
Rhine, All Along The
Romania, Taste of, Exp. Ed.
Russian Cooking, Best of, Exp. Ed.
Scandinavian Cooking, Best of
Scotland, Traditional Food From
Scottish-Irish Pub and Hearth
    Cookbook
Sephardic Israeli Cuisine
Sicilian Feasts
Slovak Cooking, Best of
Smorgasbord Cooking, Best of
South African Cookery, Traditional
South American Cookery, Art of
South Indian Cooking, Healthy
Spanish Family Cookbook, Rev. Ed.
Sri Lanka, Exotic Tastes of
Swedish, Kitchen
Swiss Cookbook, The
Syria, Taste of
Taiwanese Cuisine, Best of
Thai Cuisine, Best of Regional
Turkish Cuisine, Taste of
Ukrainian Cuisine, Best of, Exp. Ed.
Uzbek Cooking, Art of
Warsaw Cookbook, Old

Flavorful India

Treasured Recipes from a Gujarati Family

Priti Chitnis Gress

Illustrated by Chandrakant Paul W. Chitnis

HIPPOCRENE BOOKS
NEW YORK

This book is dedicated with love to all the women in my family,
and in particular
to my mother, Suvasini Patel Chitnis,
for teaching me the wonderful art of cooking and so much more,
and to my daughter, Gloria Sangita Gress,
in the hope that she will find this volume useful one day.

Book and jacket design by Acme Klong Design, Inc.
Illustrations by Chandrakant Paul W. Chitnis.

For more information, address:
HIPPOCRENE BOOKS, INC.
171 Madison Avenue
New York, NY 10016

ISBN 0-7818-1060-4
Cataloging-in-Publication Data available from the Library of Congress.
Printed in the United States of America.

Contents

Acknowledgments

First and foremost, admiration, gratitude, and love go to my mother, Suvasini Chitnis. Her own talent in the kitchen is the real inspiration behind this book. I am grateful to her for sharing her recipes and leading me through many culinary adventures. Next, I would like to thank my father, Chandrakant Paul Chitnis, for providing the beautiful illustrations that accompany this text and for sharing with me his fond memories of his own mother's kitchen. I also appreciate the support and encouragement of my husband, Jay Gress.

I would like to thank my publisher, George Blagowidow, for suggesting that I write this book, and editors, Anne E. McBride and Becca Cole for their help bringing the project together. Lastly, I'd like to thank my dear friend, Katareya Godehn, whose photography and inspired design make this book beautiful.

Introduction

I begin this cookbook with a confession: When I was a child growing up in North Carolina, I did not appreciate Indian food. My mother worked full-time and still found the opportunity to prepare fresh vegetables, dals, and curries for our family every evening. The tempting aromas from her kitchen always attracted friends and neighbors, who couldn't get enough of the delicious items she made. But being contrary children, my brother, sister, and I would beg for hamburgers or pizza instead. We didn't know what we were missing!

As I grew older, I began to enjoy Indian dishes little by little, even developing a few favorites. "Let's teach you how to cook now!" my mother encouraged. But somehow I dodged the cooking lessons. I thought it would be too complicated. Plus, she was there to cook all the foods I enjoyed.

Years later, I found myself sitting in my office in New York City with an unshakable craving for crispy Okra with Potatoes (page 69) and Yogurt Curry (page 93). Sure, there are dozens of excellent Indian restaurants in Manhattan, but none of them made these dishes like my mom did. In fact, most of them didn't even serve Gujarati specialties.

I called my mother in North Carolina, jotted down her instructions on a series of Post-it notes, and stopped at an Indian grocery store on Lexington Avenue on the way to my apartment that night. Thus began my first real foray into Indian cooking. It took me a little time to perfect my techniques, but eventually I was able to produce some of my favorite dishes and even get my mother's seal of approval on my Chicken Curry (page 101).

This cookbook is the happy result of my own culinary journey through favorite family recipes. My parents and I emigrated to the U.S. from Gujarat when I was two years old. They have kept the cooking traditions of their Indian childhood alive and pass them on to the next generation.

Even though I grew up in the U.S., I vividly remember childhood trips to India. One in particular, almost twenty-five years ago now, was special because the entire extended family was able to celebrate Christmas together. Our family is Christian, one of the religious minorities in Gujarat. We ate the holiday meal seated around my grandmother's spacious veranda. My uncles and cousins had cut a branch from a tree in the courtyard, and improvised a Christmas tree. We enjoyed steaming plates of mutton curry, cooked by my Vinu Uncle over an outdoor flame earlier that day. My aunts had been busy preparing sweet *ladvas* and fluffy puris, which were also eagerly devoured. It was a memorable holiday indeed, and very delicious food was at the center of it.

Now most of my family has emigrated to the U.S., and we still come together to celebrate weddings and birthdays and other special occasions. And of course, good food is at the heart of these gatherings. My friends all know that you cannot come to my parents' home without being fed by my mother. Most of the recipes featured here are my mother's—food she cooks everyday and for holidays and important meals. Others have been contributed by family members and friends. These are the regional specialties and everyday foods of Gujarat. Where necessary, they have been adapted to the Western kitchen. I have discovered that most Indian foods are nutritious and easy-to-prepare, not to mention tasty beyond compare, and I'm pleased to share my family's treasured recipes here.

About Gujarat

The state of Gujarat is located in western India, bounded by the Arabian Sea on the west, Pakistan to the north, the state of Rajasthan to the northeast, and Maharashtra to the south. Gujarat's name comes from Gujjar Rasthra, which translates to "the land of the Gujjars." The Gujjars were a migrant tribe that came to western India in the fifth century to escape the Huns.

Hindu kings ruled over Gujarat for several hundred years, until Mughal invaders arrived and ruled from about the eleventh century to the seventeenth century, when British rule commenced. Present-day Gujarat was formed on May 1, 1960. It is widely recognized as one of India's leading industrialized states, with textile production as one of the region's chief industries. This modernized enterprise is rooted in ancient tradition. For thousands of years, the inhabitants of Gujarat have practiced weaving, dyeing, and embroidering cloth. Visitors will find a dazzling array of folk art, from clothing to handicrafts made from wood, stone, and metal. Other important industries include chemicals and petro-chemicals (the Gujarat oil refinery complex is located near the city of Baroda). Gujarat is also India's main producer of tobacco, cotton, and groundnuts.

Most Gujaratis are Hindu and Hindu holidays are celebrated widely. One in particular, Navratri, is very popular in Gujarat. Navratri translates to "nine nights" and usually occurs in October during harvest season. Since agricultural laborers were traditionally occupied in the fields during the daytime, at night they thanked the goddesses Parvati, Lakshmi, and Sarasvati for nine nights. Three days were devoted to each goddess. Fireworks, dancing and all manner of celebration characterize this holiday in Gujarat.

Gujaratis are famous for two types of dancing: *dandiya rasa* and *garba*. The *dandiya rasa* dancers, usually men, use sticks with tiny bells *(ghungrus)* tied to the ends so that they give off a clear jingling sound when they strike one another. They dance in a circle, sometimes using an inner circle and outer circle to begin. The circles break into complicated formations. The *dandiya rasa* dancers are based on ancient Sanskrit dramas, particularly legends connected with the deity Krishna. Their origins are in harvest rituals and the circular formations that the dancers make sometimes represent the pattern of a lotus flower or other designs that are considered auspicious.

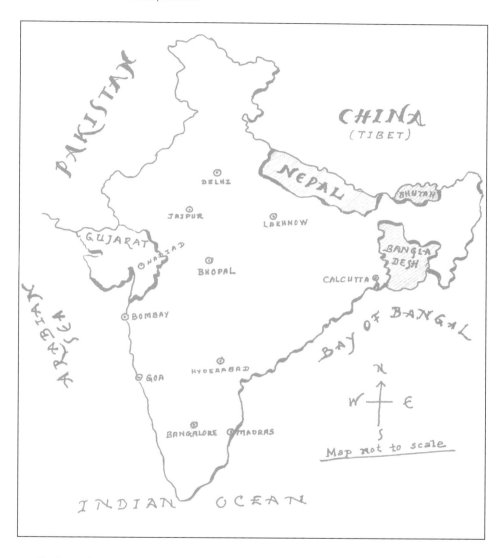

Garba is the women's counterpart to dandiya rasa and it is the most popular women's folk dance of Gujarat. It is a dance also rooted in ancient tradition, with songs that have been passed down through many generations. In many agricultural communities, the mother-goddess was worshipped in incarnations such as a painted image, a wooden structure, or even an earthen pot (garbi). In older times, the virgin girls of a village carried pots filled with sprouted corn on their heads and later immersed these pots in a river as a fertility ritual. During Navratri, village girls bearing pots *(garbis)* on their heads go from door to door and dance. A group leader sings the first line of a song and the rest repeat it in chorus. The beat is produced through clapping hands or striking sticks in unison. At every step, dancers gracefully bend sideways, their arms coming together in beautiful sweeping gestures, up and down, left and right, each movement ending in a clap.

Gujarat's Flavorful Cuisine

Gujarat is known as India's "garden state" and thus is famed for its vegetarian cuisine. A bounty of fresh vegetables—beans, eggplant, okra, tomatoes, fenugreek leaves, and many more—are delicately seasoned and served alongside creamy dals and warm chapatis.

Kitchdi, the dinnertime staple rice dish cooked with lentils, is often topped with *kadhi*, a fragrant yogurt curry that lends a rich and creamy aspect to the meal. The Gujarati *thaali* (plate) is traditionally a large stainless-steel plate containing four to six small round bowls, each filled with a different vegetarian delicacy. On the side, fresh, hot puris (puffed flatbreads), rice, pickles, and chutneys are served as accompaniments.

While the majority of Gujaratis are vegetarian Hindus, smaller populations of Muslims, Christians, and Parsis (Zoroastrians who migrated to India from Iran in the early tenth century) enjoy meat dishes. Most often they eat chicken, fish, and lamb, and avoid pork and beef. The cuisines of Muslims and Parsis have contributed to the Gujarati culinary repertoire, and no cookbook would be complete without some of their famous dishes.

These recipes span the range of Gujarati cooking, opening with a section on the snacks and appetizers that are traditionally sold by street vendors but can also be prepared at home. These include a crunchy snack mix, *dhoklas* (savory, spongy diamonds made from chickpea flour and topped with crunchy mustard seeds and shredded coconut), and a variety of potato and vegetable fritters. Next, chapters on breads and rice outline step-by-step procedures for making chapatis, puris, and rice dishes.

The chapter on vegetables is really the heart of this cookbook. Here you will find recipes for all manner of Indian vegetables, including some such as bitter gourd and fenugreek leaves, that will take some cooks into new territory altogether. Also included is a recipe for *Undhiyu*, the famous Gujarati dish of root vegetables, beans, and fenugreek dumplings.

Following that are a chapter on dals and yogurt curry *(kadhi)* and a chapter including nonvegetarian specialties like Chicken Curry and Biryani, a seasoned meat and rice casserole enjoyed throughout the state. A small chapter on chutneys and other condiments introduces cooks to specialties like Tamarind Chutney and Mango Pickle. Lastly, since a hearty, spicy meal ends best on a sweet note, a chapter on traditional sweets and beverages brings the dining experience full circle.

Guides to spices, ingredients, and utensils, along with some suggested menus, will help you navigate the Indian grocery store and prepare your own sizzling, spicy feast at home. Chronicling my mother's and family's recipes has been a very rewarding process for me. I hope this collection leads readers to a new, fresh, and flavorful adventure in Indian cooking.

Guide to Spices and Ingredients

The standard Indian spice box is a round stainless-steel container that houses seven smaller containers. I like to keep the basic staples in my spice box: ground cayenne pepper, turmeric, ground cumin, ground coriander, *garam masala*, cumin seeds, and cardamom pods. Many of the recipes in this book can be prepared with these spices alone.

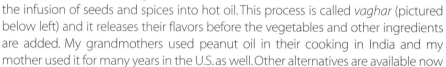

Spices will keep for several months when stored in airtight containers in a cool, dark, dry place. I like to save glass jars from pasta sauces and salsas and use those to store my spices, dals, and rice. While many of these ingredients are now available in supermarkets, you may need to visit an Asian or Indian grocery store to find some of them.

The preparation of most curries and vegetable dishes begins with the infusion of seeds and spices into hot oil. This process is called *vaghar* (pictured below left) and it releases their flavors before the vegetables and other ingredients are added. My grandmothers used peanut oil in their cooking in India and my mother used it for many years in the U.S. as well. Other alternatives are available now

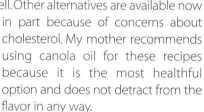

in part because of concerns about cholesterol. My mother recommends using canola oil for these recipes because it is the most healthful option and does not detract from the flavor in any way.

black mustard seeds

cumin seeds

fennel seeds

fenugreek seeds

ajwain seeds

cardamom seeds

Ajwain/Ajowan Seeds

These very tiny, pungent seeds of the lovage plant are closely related to cumin and caraway seeds but are slightly smaller. They have a strong, peppery flavor and are thus used sparingly. *Ajwain* seeds are often infused in hot oil at the beginning of preparation of a dish to impart their flavor.

Asafoetida Powder *(Hing)*

Many of the recipes in this book call for the finely ground, mustard-yellow asafoetida powder sold in small plastic containers. This spice has a powerful, even offensive smell because it contains sulfur, although the powdered version is milder than the type sold in solid lumps. Strict Hindus and Jains, who do not eat onions and garlic, often use it to flavor their dishes. Asafoetida is said to aid with digestive and respiratory problems.

Basmati Rice

This aromatic Indian rice is very popular throughout the world these days. The word *basmati* means "queen of fragrance" and this rice indeed has a delicate aroma and nutty, buttery taste. Almost all imported basmati rice is aged for six months to one year to increase its flavor. Imported basmati rice is readily available in Indian groceries in five- to fifty-five-pound bags. It should be rinsed in a couple of changes of water to release starches and remove any grit. Ideally, it should also be soaked in cold water for twenty to thirty minutes before cooking.

Bay Leaves

Dried Indian bay leaves are available whole or in pieces at Indian groceries. They have a woody fragrance and slightly pungent flavor. Look for leaves that are green and mold-free, and store them in an airtight container for up to six months.

Bengal Gram or Gram Lentils *(Channa Dal)*

This pale yellow dal is the most widely grown one in India. It is slightly larger than *toor dal*, with a stronger flavor. It should be soaked for several hours or even overnight before cooking. It is used in a variety of recipes, including vegetable dishes and sweets.

Biryani Masala

This spice mix is used to create the rice and vegetable casserole, *biryani*, and is available in small boxes at Indian groceries. One popular brand is Shan's.

Bitter Gourd/Bitter Melon *(Karela)*

This unique vegetable resembles a cucumber with very bumpy skin. It has a pale, firm flesh and a very bitter taste. Look for bright green, young bitter gourds (the skin gets yellow with age) at the Indian grocery store. The skin is peeled and the interior flesh with seeds is eaten. Cooked bitter gourd is said to stimulate the appetite, cleanse the liver, and purify the blood.

Bottle Gourd *(Doodhi)*

This pale green gourd has a broad base and narrow stem. It has a smooth skin and tastes similar to summer squash. It's best to buy slightly unripe, small gourds, about ten inches or so in length. Unripe gourds have a softer, papery skin and the older ones develop a tough, woody shell. They have immature seeds and a softer skin. As the gourd ages, the skin toughens and the

seeds need to be removed. Chunks of this gourd are added to dals and vegetable dishes. It is also used in desserts because of its sweet, mild flavor.

Cardamom *(Elaichi)*

Fragrant cardamom pods are a staple in most Gujarati kitchens. The aromatic seeds inside the pod lend a rich, sweet essence to teas and desserts, but are also used in savory dishes and to flavor rice while it cooks. Cardamom is available in smaller green pods or larger, wrinkled black pods. The recipes in this book use green pods. Cardamom is also available in powdered form and some stores sell whole seeds. I recommend buying whole pods as the crushed version loses its flavor quickly. To remove the seeds, roast the pods in a dry pan over low heat for a few minutes. When cooled, split the pods open and carefully remove the seeds. You can use a spice grinder or mortar and pestle to crush them.

Cardamom is said to aid in digestion and help relieve stomach pains. Some people even use cardamom-flavored tea for headaches, and gargle with cardamom-infused water to soothe sore throats. Indian emperors chewed cardamom pods to freshen their mouth after a meal.

Cayenne/Red Chili Powder *(Lal Marchu)*
This hot red pepper powder is made from chilies that are dried and then ground to a fine powder. The color of the powder ranges from reddish-orange to dark red, depending on the type of chilies used. India is actually the largest exporter of cayenne pepper and it is utilized in almost all savory dishes and curries. This spice gives food its heat, so feel free to adjust the amount in recipes according to personal preference. Foods cooked with cayenne pepper, particularly soups, curries, and dals, can help to clear sinuses when you have a cold.

Chapati or *Atta* Flour

This special whole wheat flour is stone ground and made from low-gluten wheat. It is a light tan color with a soft texture that makes it easier to knead and roll flatbreads that cook quickly. Regular whole wheat flour should not be used for Indian flatbreads. In a pinch, you can substitute two parts white all-purpose flour to one part whole wheat flour.

Chat Masala
Chat means "to lick" in Gujarati and Hindi. This tangy, salty spice blend, which gets its distinctive flavor from black salt, green mango powder, and ground cumin, is used to season many finger-licking good snacks and foods. *Chat masala* is available in Indian groceries in 3.5-ounce packages.

Chickpea Flour *(Besan)*
This is a yellowish, high-protein flour with a nutty, rich flavor. It can be used in sauces and curries as a thickening agent, but is also used to make batters for various fried snacks and fritters.

Cinnamon *(Taj)*
Cinnamon sticks are available in most supermarkets and Indian groceries. Their sweet, woody scent adds a tempting aroma and unique flavor to rice, curries, meat dishes, and desserts. Look for cinnamon that is not chipped and sticks that

are long and whole. Cinnamon is thought to be effective in treatment of colds and nausea.

Coconut *(Nariyal)*

Indian grocery stores sell whole coconuts, dried flaked coconut, finely powdered coconut, and coconut milk. Dried coconut flakes are typically used in chutneys, salads and desserts. Powdered coconut is available in various sized plastic bags, usually in the same aisle as the nuts. It is used to flavor savory and sweet dishes. Canned coconut milk is a popular addition to make curries sweeter and creamier.

Coriander *(Dhana)*

Coriander is an aromatic herb with flat, fan-shaped leaves. Cilantro, the leaf form of the herb, is found in supermarkets and Indian grocery stores and used as a flavorful garnish in many of these recipes. Coriander seeds and ground coriander are readily available in Indian groceries. Whole or crushed seeds bring a sweet, lemony flavor to dals, curries, biryani, and pickles. Ground coriander is used in most recipes in this book. It is an essential component of many spice mixtures and curries.

Cumin *(Jeeru)*

A key ingredient in many curries and vegetable dishes, cumin is available as whole seeds and in powdered form. With its peppery, bittersweet flavor, cumin is used in the preparation of dishes across India. In Gujarat, ground cumin is combined with ground coriander to create dhana-jeeru, a favorite spice blend. Cumin is praised for its ability to aid with digestion. In fact, yogurt sprinkled with cumin powder is favorite digestive dish.

Curry Leaves *(Kadhi Patta)*

These fragrant leaves are usually sold dried in Indian grocery stores but are sometimes available fresh as well. They lend a unique, lingering aroma to vegetarian dishes, and particularly to the famous Gujarati yogurt curry. Curry leaves are used for flavoring dishes but are removed before eating. They are dark green, almond-shaped, and have a strong, currylike odor.

Curry leaves are also used in Ayurvedic medicine. They can be crushed into a paste to aid with skin irritations and insect bites. Drinking the juice of curry leaves with lemon juice and sugar is also said to aid with digestive problems. On another interesting note, curry leaves are sometimes boiled and combined with coconut oil and then rubbed into the scalp to promote hair growth and prevent graying.

ENO Fruit Salt

This fruit salt is a combination of citric acid and sodium bicarbonate. It is made in India and is generally available at Indian grocery stores and health food stores in small-gram bottles. It is popularly used as an antacid in India. Baking soda can be substituted.

Fennel Seeds

These are the bright green, small, cylindrical seeds of the fennel plant (a large, dill-like, bulbous plant with tiny, yellow flowers). The seeds have a sweet, intense, licorice-like flavor. In India, fennel-infused water is used to treat colic in babies.

Fenugreek *(Methi)*

Fenugreek is available as a leafy plant, as seeds, and in ground form. The recipes in this book call for fenugreek leaves in fresh, dried, or frozen form, and for fenugreek seeds. Fenugreek leaves are sometimes available fresh at Indian grocery stores, but you can also find them dried and frozen. The leaves and seeds have a strong, currylike odor and are widely used in Indian cooking.

Fenugreek is also believed to aid in a variety of ailments, including flatulence, coughing, and diabetes. The seeds also promote lactation and are fed to cows to increase their milk supply.

Flaked Rice *(Pawa)*

These rice grains have been flattened by large rollers until they are extremely thin. They are small, oblong, flat, and grayish in color. Flaked rice is often used in snack mixes.

Garam Masala

This famous spice combination has found its way to tables around the world. Each region of India differs in the ingredients used to produce *garam masala*, and indeed families and individual cooks have their own combinations, but *garam masala* powder usually consists of a combination of cardamom, bay leaves, cumin seeds, coriander seeds, black peppercorns, cinnamon, and cloves. *Garam masala* yields a slightly sweet flavor to many Indian dishes and is often used as a topping or additional flavoring.

You can find prepared *garam masala* powder in Indian grocery stores, or you can make your own at home. Here is a basic recipe:

2 bay leaves	2 teaspoons cumin seeds
1 (1-inch) stick cinnamon	1 teaspoon coriander seeds
1 teaspoon black peppercorns	1 teaspoon whole cloves
1 teaspoon cardamom seeds	

Combine all the ingredients in a spice grinder or blender and process until powdered. Store in an airtight container. This mixture will keep its flavor for several weeks.

Makes $^1/_2$ cup

Garlic-Ginger Paste *(Adu Lasarn)*

You are likely to find this simple but powerful paste in almost any Gujarati kitchen. It consists of fresh garlic and ginger ground together into a paste. It is easy to make a big batch that can be kept on hand in the refrigerator. Here is a basic recipe:

> **2 heads of garlic, peeled**
> **$^2/_3$ cup (4-6 ounces) peeled, chopped (into $^1/_2$-inch chunks) fresh ginger**
>
> Combine these ingredients in a blender or food processor and process until a smooth paste forms. Add 1 tablespoon of water, a few drops at a time, if necessary. Store in a glass jar with a tightly fitting lid in the refrigerator for up to three months.
> **Makes 1$^1/_2$ cups**

Ghee (Clarified Butter)

Ghee, considered since ancient times to be "liquid gold," has long been a symbol of wealth in India. It is made from unsalted butter and is available in all Indian grocery stores, sold in tins or glass jars in the refrigerated section. Its sweet, nutty taste adds richness to many Indian dishes. It is often spread on freshly cooked flatbreads to give them softness and flavor. You can make your own ghee at home with this simple recipe:

> **1 pound (4 sticks) unsalted butter**   Melt the butter in a heavy-bottomed medium-size pan over medium heat. When the butter begins to boil, reduce the heat to low and simmer for about 15 minutes, uncovered. Keep a close eye on it to avoid burning. Use a wooden spoon to remove some of the foam on top. The ghee should be a clear, golden color. Remove from the heat and cool slightly. Pour it through a fine sieve or cheesecloth into a glass jar with a tightly fitting lid. This clarified butter will keep for 3 to 4 weeks at room temperature and up to 6 months refrigerated.
> **Makes about 2 cups**

Ghilora (Tindora)

These are also known as Indian cucumbers or gherkins. They are little, two- to three-inch squash with pale green, vertical stripes and have a mild zucchini-like flavor. Select small, firm *ghilora* without wrinkles. They will keep in the refrigerator in a paper bag for about four to five days.

Green Chilies *(Lila Marcha)*

These slim, finger-length peppers are available at Indian grocery stores. Generally speaking, the smaller and greener a chili, the hotter it will be. These are hot but will not burn your tongue off. Use them according to taste in these recipes. The ripened version, red chilies, are also available fresh and dried.

Gur

This palm sugar is made from the sap of coconut, date, and sugar palms. *Gur* is sold as cloth-wrapped loaves, small half-rounds, cylinders, or cakes, or in tubs. To get it out of the tub, dip a heavy-duty spoon in hot water and use it to scoop the sugar out. *Gur* should be refrigerated in an airtight container or plastic wrap and used within six months of purchase.

Lemongrass *(Bhustrina)*

Fragrant fresh lemongrass stalks are sold in bunches at Indian and Asian grocery stores. They have a pale, greenish-yellow color and clean, lemony smell. Fresh lemongrass will keep in the refrigerator for one to two weeks. Lemongrass is considered to be a diuretic and tonic and is used to flavor the famous Indian tea, *Masala Chai.*

Long Green Beans *(Chora)*

These Indian-style green beans are much longer and a bit thinner than their western counterparts. Trim the ends and cut into $1^1/_2$-inch pieces for cooking. They will keep in the refrigerator for four to five days in a paper bag. Available at Indian grocery stores.

Mango Pulp *(Keri No Rus)*

This thick, orange syrup is made from the very sweet pulp of mangoes. It is delicious served with a little cardamom powder and sipped directly or served over ice cream and rice pudding. It is sold in large cans at Indian groceries.

Mung Beans *(Dal)*

These are whole, tiny, oval beans with green skins, or split *mung dal* without skins, which are flat and light yellow. Mung beans are sometimes used for sprouting or to prepare thick dals.

Mustard Seeds *(Rai)*

There are three main types of mustard seeds: black, white, and brown. The recipes in this book call for black mustard seeds, which are available in Indian groceries. When infused in hot oil, they impart a strong, acrid flavor. This method of frying mustard seeds until they crackle is the first step in many Indian recipes. In India, mustard is believed to ward off evil, and some Indian mothers keep away malignant spirits by making a wish over their children with a handful of mustard seeds.

Papdi Beans *(Valor)*

These broad beans resemble snap peas and have light-green, flattish, slightly curved pods, which contain small seeds. They are usually available fresh at Indian groceries but may be frozen as well. The tough stem/string needs to be removed before cooking.

Poppy Seeds *(Khus Khus)*

Indian poppy seeds differ from European ones in that they are ivory to beige in color. These tiny, grainy seeds provide a unique texture and flavor to many Indian dishes. They are available in plastic packets at Indian grocery stores and should be stored in airtight containers in the refrigerator.

Potatoes (Bataka)

Most of these recipes can be prepared with a variety of potatoes. Generally, baking potatoes work well. If using other types, like red potatoes or Yukon Gold, please note that they may require a shorter cooking time.

Puffed Rice *(Mumra)*

Puffed rice is used mainly in crunchy snack mixes. It resembles pale, slightly translucent Rice Krispies, and is usually available in fourteen-ounce bags.

Red Lentils *(Masoor Dal)*

The lentil recipes in this book call for split red lentils. They have a delicate, nutty flavor and cook very quickly. They require no soaking beforehand, just rinsing. They become golden-yellow when cooked and add nutritional value and flavor to rice and vegetable dishes.

Rice Flour (Chaval ka Atta)
This powdery white flour resembles grainy sand. It is mainly used to thicken sauces and to make doughs and batters. Rice flour should be stored in airtight containers and used within four months of purchase.

Rose Essence (Gulab Jal)
Made from the petals of damask roses, this is the diluted form of pure rose oil. Its sweet, floral scent make it a perfect ingredient for desserts and drinks. Culinary rose essence (check label; many other rose oils are for external use only) is usually available in one-ounce bottles.

Saffron (Kesar)
This expensive and precious spice is available in most supermarkets as well as in Indian groceries. It is sold in loosely matted, dark orange strands and used sparingly in recipes to provide flavor and color. Powdered saffron should be avoided since it is sometimes combined with turmeric and therefore of inferior quality. It is often soaked in warm water or milk beforehand and then poured into a dish to add richness and fragrance. Saffron is believed to be a powerful aphrodisiac. In India it is also used as a paste to paint a religious mark on the forehead.

Sesame Seeds (Tal)
Sesame seeds are tiny, glossy, tan-color seeds with a sweet, nutty flavor. They are used in Indian sweets.

Sev Noodles
These thin chickpea noodle bits are yellow to orange in color and about the thickness of capellini or spaghetti. Some varieties are available flavored, but plain sev is also used for snack mix recipes.

Surti Papdi Lilva (Indian Green Kidney Beans)
These are plump, broad pods filled with pale greenish-yellow beans. The recipes in this book call for these interior beans, which are usually available frozen and canned at Indian grocery stores.

Tamarind Concentrate (Pani Puri Paste)
This jellylike, dark brown paste is available in plastic tubs in Indian grocery stores. It is made from the pulp of the Indian tamarind tree and has a sweet, tart, fruity taste. This concentrate is used in curries, soups, and dals, and especially to make tamarind chutney.

Tandoori Paste

Jars of this popular, vivid red cooking paste are often available in regular super-markets these days but always available in Indian groceries. One popular brand is Patak's. This paste gives tandoori chicken its bright red color and delicious flavor. Unused paste should be refrigerated after a jar is opened.

Toor Dal (Yellow Lentils)

Toor dal is the mostly widely used dal in India. These pale yellow to golden-color lentils are sold skinned and split into two rounds. It is available dry or oiled. The oiled variety is coated with castor oil as a preservative. Both varieties should be soaked in hot water and thoroughly rinsed before use, but take particular care to rinse the oily ones. *Toor dal* has a pleasant, nutty taste and cooks relatively quick-ly. It should be soaked for an hour or two before cooking.

Turia (Rough Okra, Ridged Gourd, or Silk Squash)

This squash is a member of the cucumber family. It is about eight to twelve inches long with long, spiny ridges that must be peeled off. It has a buttery, soft flesh with a zucchini-like flavor. Select small, firm squash without dark spots. Refrigerate in a paper or plastic bag, and use within a couple of days.

Turmeric *(Hardar)*

One of the most frequently used spices in the Indian kitchen, turmeric imparts a rich yellow color and a distinct earthy flavor to many dishes. Interestingly, it is also revered in the Ayurvedic tradition for its healing properties. A turmeric paste can be prepared and used to treat minor cuts and burns because of its antiseptic properties. Turmeric paste is also a cooling, soothing remedy for sore muscles. In some families, brides and grooms are bathed in a turmeric paste to improve their complexions before the wedding day. Recipes in this book call for turmeric pow-der. Be careful handling the powder as it easily stains hands and clothes!

Tuver Lilva (Indian Pigeon Peas)

Tuver beans are short, green pods filled with tender pigeon peas. The recipes in this book call for the interior pigeon peas, which are usually available in frozen packages or canned at Indian grocery stores.

Urad Dal (Black Lentils)

These lentils are available with skins and without. The recipes in this book call for split or skinless lentils. They have a flourlike aroma and mild taste. They do not require soaking as they cook quickly.

Guide to Utensils
and Equipment

A Trip through the Traditional Gujarati Kitchen

Here are some of my father's drawings and memories from his mother's kitchen in 1940s and '50s Gujarat.

Ceramic jars were used to store mango and lemon pickles, which were made when those fruits were in season. A mortar and pestle was used to make freshly ground spices that provided foods with the most robust flavor.

My father recalls seeing his mother prepare fresh chapatis with a *velan* (thin rolling pin) and *patli* (round wooden block) in the mornings as he was getting ready for school. Many times, he would carry lunch to his older sister, who worked as a nurse at the hospital, in a tiffin. This marvelous stainless-steel lunch box held separate containers for vegetables, rice, dal, or any other hot food. In larger cities like Ahmedabad, you can still hire tiffin-runners to carry hot lunches from home to office workers.

Large containers such as this one would hold several months' supply of rice, dal, and wheat. On Saturday mornings, my father and his brothers and sisters would help their mother sort through an enormous pile of wheat, picking out any grit or stones from the field. After that, his older brothers would take the clean grain to a nearby mill for grinding.

Here are some essential kitchen utensils. From left to right, the first is a slotted spoon called a *zaro*, used for deep-frying foods like puffed puri breads and vegetable fritters *(bhajias)*. The second is a *tabetho*, and it is used for flipping pan-cooked flatbreads, such as chapatis. The third is an Indian-style set of tongs called a *sansi*. It is used to hold hot pots and carry them off the stove. The last is a wooden spoon, or *chatro*, traditionally used to make yogurt curry.

In the Indian kitchen, the *paniyar* was the area where water *(pani)* was kept. Sometimes the water was only turned on a couple of times a day by the local authority, so it had to be stored in large clay pots called *matlas*. People used the long-handled *doya* to get water from the pot and fill their glasses.

No Indian kitchen would be complete without a mortar and pestle, called a *khandadio* and *sambelu* in Gujarati. Everything from grains to spices to dried chili peppers were crushed with this utensil for use in cooking.

This set of grinding stones is called a *ghanti*. My grandmother used this to crush roasted seeds and make her own ground cumin and coriander. It could also be used to grind dried chickpeas into superior-tasting flour.

Most Indian kitchens had a special place for the teakettle and teacups, such as the shelf pictured here.

This "Primus" kerosene stove was prized in Indian households because the flame could very easily be adjusted to different temperatures. Young brides loved to receive a stove like this as a wedding gift. Once natural gas was widely available, the popularity of this stove declined some, but my grandmother still preferred to use hers to whip up quick items like tea, omelets, and puris.

These are the typical water pots used for storing water in the kitchen.

Useful Equipment

Here are some items that you will find useful in preparing the recipes in this book:

Heavy-bottomed stainless-steel saucepans, skillets, and pots: You can prepare most of the recipes in this book with regular heavy pots and pans.

Blender or food processor: Here is the modern answer to the old-fashioned grinding stones and mortars and pestles! A blender or food processor is nice to have for making garlic-ginger paste, puréeing onions, grinding nuts, and making chutneys, among many other things.

Hand blender: This is especially helpful for puréeing dal to a creamy consistency. While handy, this item is not essential.

Spice grinder or coffee mill: This is a nice item to have to make freshly ground spices in small quantities. In a pinch, you could use a larger blender or food processor. Accessories like a small container attachment are now available for many blenders and are a perfect substitute for a spice grinder.

Rolling pin: The Indian-style rolling pin is called a *velan*. It is thinner than the typical Western rolling pin and is made in one piece. The wider center and tapered ends make it perfect for making very flat chapatis and other breads. They are available for purchase at Indian grocery stores.

Wooden board: In India, breads are rolled out on a round wooden surface called a *patli*. While most wooden work surfaces can be substituted, a *patli* is the perfect space for making chapatis and other flatbreads as it helps make their round shape. They are also available at Indian grocery stores.

Skillet: The Indian *tawa* is a flat, lightweight iron or steel skillet with a wooden handle. It is used for cooking chapatis and other flatbreads evenly on the stove. They are also available in nonstick varieties at many Indian grocery stores. You can substitute a nonstick frying pan, cast-iron skillet, or griddle.

Deep-frying pan: The Indian *kadhai* is similar to a wok. It has a deep, curved bottom that helps distribute heat very quickly and evenly as you deep-fry fritters, puris, and other items. *Kadhais* are available at Indian groceries in stainless-steel, carbon-steel, and cast-iron varieties. A wok or any shallow pot appropriate for frying can be substituted.

Snacks and Appetizers

Crunchy Snack Rounds

Dhebra

Dhebra are a snack favorite at our family table. They are best enjoyed warm with chutney. This recipe, from my mother's friend Indu Makwana, uses a combination of different flours to give the snack its unique texture. Rice flour lends it crispness while white cornmeal gives it softness. Indu Auntie notes that you can also add one-third cup creamed corn, drained and ground, for additional moistness.

---

1 cup buckwheat *(bajri)* flour

1 cup chapati flour

$1/4$ cup rice flour

$1/4$ cup white cornmeal

$1/4$ cup chickpea *(besan)* flour

$1/8$ cup uncooked Cream of Wheat

$1 1/2$ tablespoons garlic-ginger paste

$1/3$ cup chopped fenugreek leaves (fresh or frozen)

$2/3$ teaspoon *ajwain* seeds

$1/2$ teaspoon ground cayenne pepper

$1/2$ teaspoon turmeric

$1/4$ teaspoon ground cumin

$1/4$ teaspoon ground coriander

1 teaspoon finely chopped green chili

1 teaspoon salt

$1/4$ cup oil

$1/2$ cup plain yogurt

2 teaspoons sesame seeds

Combine all the ingredients in a large bowl. Mix well with a spoon and then use your hands to knead it into a thick dough. This will take 2 to 3 minutes. Add 1 to 2 additional teaspoons of yogurt if necessary.

Divide the dough into ten patties about $3/4$ inch thick and 2 inches in diameter. Roll out each patty with a rolling pin to about 5 inches in diameter. Heat a *tawa* (page 25) or nonstick skillet over medium heat. Add the first *dhebra*, cook for 15 to 20 seconds, and flip. Add a few drops of oil around the edges of the *dhebra* and flip every few seconds. Remove from the heat when well browned, about 1 to 2 minutes.

Continue to roll out and cook the *dhebras*, collecting them on a plate lined with paper towels.

Savory Diamonds

Khaman Dhokla

Makes about 25 diamonds

These spongy treats are made from fermented chickpeas and are one of Gujarat's most famous culinary offerings. They are a delicious afternoon snack or even a breakfast treat. This recipe requires steaming. You can use a large pot or wok with a cover that will fit a stainless-steel Indian plate *(thali)* within. The plates are usually about twelve inches in diameter and one and a half inches high, perfect for making this snack. You can usually purchase these plates at Indian grocery stores. If you are using smaller plates, you may need two. Just be sure it is one and a half inches high.

Note: This recipe requires about 20 hours of fermentation time.

2 cups chana dal	1 teaspoon ENO fruit salt or baking soda
1/2 cup yogurt	1 tablespoon oil
2 tablespoons garlic-ginger paste	2 teaspoons black mustard seeds
1 teaspoon salt	1/4 cup chopped fresh cilantro
2 teaspoons sugar	2 tablespoons unsweetened coconut flakes
1 teaspoon turmeric	
2 green chilies, finely chopped (or to taste)	

 Wash the dal and place it in a medium-size bowl. Add enough warm water to cover the dal by 1 inch. Cover and leave overnight or 8 hours.

Drain the dal and place in a blender or food processor. Process until it forms a paste.

Combine the dal with the yogurt, garlic-ginger paste, salt, sugar, turmeric, and chilies. Mix well. Cover and allow the batter to ferment on a countertop for 12 hours.

Prepare the steaming apparatus: Heat 2 cups of water in the bottom of a pot or wok and, with a little oil, grease the plate you will be using.

In a small bowl, combine $1^1/_2$ cups of the batter with $^1/_2$ teaspoon of the ENO. Stir well. It is important to add the ENO just before the batter will be steamed so that it is active. It should be frothy and bubbling.

Spread the ENO batter on the greased plate. Carefully use tongs to place the plate over the steaming water. Cover with a lid. Steam for 20 to 30 minutes, depending on the size of the plate used. The *khaman dhokla* will be done when a knife inserted comes out clean.

Combine the remaining $^1/_2$ teaspoon of the ENO with the remaining batter and repeat the steaming process. When the *khaman dhokla* has cooled, cut it into 2-inch diamonds or squares.

Heat the oil in a small skillet over medium heat. Add the mustard seeds and sauté for 3 to 4 minutes, until the seeds pop and turn brown. Sprinkle this oil mixture over the *khaman* pieces, with the cilantro and coconut.

Spicy Dumplings in Yogurt Sauce

Dahi Vada

Makes 4 appetizer servings
(about 3 to 4 patties apiece)

This is a popular street food in Gujarat. The cool yogurt sauce complements the spicy patties, which are made from a combination of *urad dal* and *mung dal*. You can use green chili for a hotter version or substitute bell pepper for a milder version. Either way, it is a hearty, filling, and tasty snack. Please note that this recipe requires soaking the dal for at least six hours or overnight.

For the dumplings:	For the yogurt sauce:
1 cup *urad dal*	1 cup plain yogurt, beaten smooth with a whisk
$^1/_4$ cup *mung dal*	$^1/_4$ to 1 teaspoon ground cayenne pepper, according to taste
$1^1/_2$ teaspoons garlic-ginger paste	$^1/_4$ teaspoon black pepper
5 to 10 peppercorns, according to taste	1 teaspoon salt
$^1/_2$ to 1 green chili, or $^1/_4$ cup chopped green bell pepper, according to taste	1 teaspoon sugar
1 cup oil for deep-frying	
	For garnish:
	2 tablespoons chopped fresh cilantro

 Combine the *urad dal* and *mung dal* in a large bowl and add enough water to cover by about $^1/_2$ inch. Cover and soak for 6 hours up to overnight.

Drain the dal and place it in a blender or food processor with the garlic-ginger paste, peppercorns, and green chili. Process until completely blended and forms a slightly coarse mixture. (Note: The mixture should be coarse and somewhat firm, not liquid like batter.)

Oil your hands and work with 1 tablespoon of the dal mixture at a time to form twelve to sixteen small balls. Heat the oil in a *kadhai* or pan appropriate for deep-frying. Flatten each ball slightly into a patty-shaped dumpling, and deep-fry 4 to 8 dumplings at a time, until golden brown, about 1 minute.

Flavorful India

Fill a container that is big enough to hold all the fried dumplings with about 1 inch of warm water. Add the fried dumplings to the water and soak for 30 seconds to 1 minute. Drain the water and with your hands, gently squeeze out any excess from each dumpling.

To prepare the yogurt sauce, thoroughly combine the yogurt, red pepper, black pepper, salt, and sugar.

Place the dumplings in the yogurt sauce and garnish with cilantro. Serve with Tamarind Chutney (page 119).

Sesame-Nutmeg Squares

Sukhdi

Makes 16 to 18 squares

These snacks become quite crunchy once they harden. They are an excellent accompaniment to afternoon tea or coffee.

---

1 cup ghee or (2 sticks) butter	1/4 cup sesame seeds
2 cups whole wheat or chapati flour	1 cup *gur* (Indian brown sugar)
1 tablespoon fennel seeds	2 tablespoons milk
1/2 teaspoon nutmeg	

Grease a 9 x 13-inch pan.

Heat 1/2 the ghee in a large nonstick skillet over medium-low heat. Add the flour and stir constantly until the ghee is absorbed and the flour is roasted, about 4 to 5 minutes.

Roast the fennel seeds in a small skillet over low heat for 4 to 5 minutes, or on a tray in a 300ºF oven for 5 to 10 minutes, until brown. Lightly crush the fennel seeds and add them, with the nutmeg and sesame seeds, to the flour mixture. Mix thoroughly.

In a bowl, combine the remaining ghee with the *gur* and milk.

Over low heat, slowly add the *gur* mixture to the flour mixture, stirring constantly. Continue to cook, stirring constantly for about 5 minutes.

Spread the mixture in the prepared pan. Press firmly with a spatula to even the mixture out and set it. Cut it into sixteen to eighteen pieces while the mixture is still warm. It will harden as it cools.

Crunchy Snack Mix

Bhel Puri

This spicy, savory snack mix gets flavor and texture from a variety of elements. *Sev* are very thin, crispy chickpea noodle bits (see page 20) available in Indian groceries. Puffed rice cereal can be substituted for the *mumra*, in a pinch. The snack mix is eaten topped with chutneys and yogurt.

2 tablespoons oil	1 small onion, very finely chopped
1 teaspoon black mustard seeds	1 medium-size tomato, diced
1 teaspoon cumin seeds	$3/4$ cup pomegranate seeds
$1/2$ teaspoon turmeric	1 cup green mango, cubed
$1/4$ teaspoon asafoetida powder	$1/2$ cup Cilantro Chutney (page 118)
2 cups puffed rice *(mumra)*	$1/2$ cup Tamarind Chutney (page 119)
10 puris (page 50 or store-bought), in bite-size pieces	$1/2$ cup plain yogurt
2 cups *sev* noodles	
1 small potato, boiled, peeled, and cubed	

 Heat the oil in a large pot over medium-low heat. Add the mustard seeds and cumin seeds. When the seeds begin to pop and turn brown, add the turmeric and asafoetida powder. Stir well. Add the puffed rice, puri pieces, and *sev* noodles. Stir well to coat with the spices. Transfer the mixture to a large bowl. Add the potato, onion, tomato, pomegranate seeds, and mango. Stir well.

Serve the snack mix with Cilantro Chutney, Tamarind Chutney, and yogurt in small bowls alongside as toppings.

Mashed Potato Puffs

Bataka Vada

Makes about 30 potato balls

Here are two slightly different recipes for the potato filling in this appetizer. The first is slightly spicier with more red pepper and garlic-ginger paste. The second is slightly sweeter. Both are equally delicious. These potato puffs are a perfect afternoon snack, party hors d'oeuvre, or first course. Serve them hot with chutney on the side for dipping.

Spicy Potato Filling:

3 large potatoes, boiled, peeled, and mashed

1 tablespoon coarsely chopped cashews

1 tablespoon golden raisins

1 teaspoon sesame seeds

$1/4$ to $1/2$ teaspoon ground cayenne pepper

$1/8$ teaspoon turmeric

$1/4$ teaspoon ground cumin

$1/4$ teaspoon ground coriander

$1/2$ teaspoon garlic-ginger paste

$1/2$ teaspoon salt

1 teaspoon lemon juice

1 green chili, finely chopped (optional)

2 tablespoons finely chopped fresh cilantro

Mild Potato Filling:

3 large potatoes, boiled, peeled and mashed

1 tablespoon coarsely chopped cashews

1 tablespoon golden raisins

1 teaspoon sesame seeds

Pinch ground cayenne pepper

$1/8$ teaspoon turmeric

$1/2$ teaspoon salt

$1/2$ teaspoon sugar

$1/2$ green chili, finely chopped (optional)

2 tablespoons finely chopped fresh cilantro

For the batter:

1 cup chickpea flour *(besan)*

$1/4$ teaspoon ground cayenne pepper

$1/4$ teaspoon turmeric

$1/2$ teaspoon salt

For deep-frying:

$1^{1}/2$ cups oil

 Combine your choice of the potato filling ingredients in a medium-size bowl, mashing it well with your hands. Form the potato mixture into about thirty small balls approximately 1 inch in diameter.

Combine the batter ingredients in a small bowl. Slowly add $2/3$ cup of water, a few tablespoons at a time, mixing well with a spoon.

Heat the oil over medium-high heat in a *kadhai* (see page 25) or pan appropriate for deep-frying. Dip each potato ball in the batter, shake off the excess, and fry batches of 4 to 8 in the oil until golden brown, about 1 to 2 minutes.

Drain the potato balls in a bowl lined with paper towels to absorb excess oil. Serve hot.

Potato Fritters

These fritters are a classic snack served with afternoon tea. In India, they are sold hot by street vendors. You can substitute other sturdy vegetables for the potatoes, including thick slices of white mushroom, onion, or sweet potatoes.

For the batter:

2 cups chickpea flour *(besan)*

1 tablespoon rice flour

1/2 to 1 teaspoon ground cayenne pepper

1/2 teaspoon turmeric

1/2 teaspoon ground cumin

1/2 teaspoon ground coriander

1 teaspoon salt

1/8 teaspoon asafoetida powder

1 tablespoon garlic-ginger paste

1 tablespoon coriander seeds, lightly crushed

1 teaspoon black peppercorns, crushed

1 teaspoon baking powder

1/4 cup chopped fresh cilantro

1/2 to 1 green chili, minced

1/2 cup plain yogurt

2 cups oil for deep-frying

4 medium-size potatoes, peeled and sliced (1/8-inch thick)

Combine all the batter ingredients in a medium-size bowl. Stir well. Slowly add 1/4 to 1/2 cup of warm water and continue stirring until a thick batter forms.

Heat the oil in a deep pan or *kadhai* over medium-low heat. Add 2 tablespoons of the hot oil to the batter mixture. Stir well.

Dip the potato slices in the batter and then fry in the hot oil, a few at a time, for about 2 minutes, turning midway, until golden brown. Drain on paper towels and serve hot.

Potato Samosas

Makes 10 to 12 samosas

Vegetarian samosas are enjoyed throughout Gujarat. They make an excellent appetizer when served with Cilantro Chutney (page 118) or Tamarind Chutney (page 119). Your guests will appreciate your efforts!

For the filling:

1 tablespoon oil

$^1/_2$ medium onion, chopped ($^1/_4$ cup)

$1^1/_2$ teaspoons garlic-ginger paste

$^1/_2$ cup chopped fresh cilantro

$^1/_4$ cup chopped fresh mint

1 to 2 tablespoons finely chopped fresh green chili (to taste)

1 teaspoon salt

$^1/_2$ cup cooked green peas

3 medium-size potatoes, boiled, peeled and mashed

For the dough:

$1^1/_2$ cups chapati flour

1 teaspoon salt

3 tablespoons oil

2 cups oil for deep-frying

To prepare the filling, heat the oil in a skillet over medium heat. Add the onions and sauté for 3 to 5 minutes, until lightly browned. Reduce the heat to medium-low, and add the garlic-ginger paste, cilantro, mint, and green chili. Sauté for 1 to 2 minutes. Add the salt, peas, and potatoes. Stir well to combine. Remove from the heat and set aside.

To prepare the dough, combine the flour, salt, and oil in a bowl. Mix well with your hands. Slowly add $^1/_2$ cup of water, a few tablespoons at a time, and knead into a dough that is firm, springy, and not sticky.

To assemble the samosas, divide dough into 10 to 12 walnut-size balls. With a rolling pin, roll out a ball of dough into a circle about 6 inches in diameter. Place $1^1/_2$ tablespoons of stuffing on the top half of the circle. Fold the bottom half up to form a semicircle. Bring the sides around to make a triangle. Dip your fingers in water and run them along the edges to wet them; press together to seal firmly. Continue with the remaining dough balls and filling.

Heat 2 cups of oil in a deep pan or *kadhai* over medium-low heat. When the oil is hot, add the samosas, two or three at a time, and deep-fry for 2 to 3 minutes, turning midway, until golden brown. Collect the fried samosas in a bowl lined with paper towels. Serve hot.

Channa Dal Potato Patties

Potato Tikka

This recipe requires some extra time as the *channa dal* (Bengal Gram, see page 13) must be soaked for two hours. The delicious result is well worth it though! These spicy pan-fried patties are wonderful snacks or appetizers and can be enjoyed plain or served with chutney.

---

2 tablespoons *channa dal* (without skins)

3 tablespoons plus 1 1/2 teaspoons oil

1/4 teaspoon cumin seeds

1/4 teaspoon black mustard seeds

Pinch of asafoetida powder

1 teaspoon finely grated fresh ginger

1/2 teaspoon very finely chopped green chili pepper

1/2 teaspoon ground cayenne pepper

1/8 teaspoon turmeric

1/2 teaspoon *chat masala* (see page 14)

1/4 teaspoon *garam masala*

1/4 teaspoon salt (or more to taste)

3 medium-size potatoes, peeled, boiled, and mashed

1/4 cup green peas, parboiled and coarsely mashed

1 teaspoon finely chopped fresh cilantro

 Soak the *channa dal* in enough warm water to cover by 2 inches, for 2 hours. Drain, leaving about 1 1/2 teaspoons of water. Place the mixture in a blender or food processor and process for 1 to 2 minutes, or until coarsely ground.

Heat 1 1/2 teaspoons of the oil in a medium-size skillet. Add the cumin seeds. When the cumin seeds are browned, add the mustard seeds and asafoetida powder. Cover to avoid splattering. Add the ginger, green chili, cayenne, turmeric, *chat masala*, *garam masala*, and salt. Stir well for 1 minute. Add the potatoes and stir until coated with the spices and heated through. Remove from the heat.

Add the *channa dal* mixture to the potatoes along with the peas and cilantro. Stir well to combine.

Form the mixture into fifteen to twenty 1- to 2-inch balls. Flatten each ball into a patty with your palm (oil your hands if necessary).

Heat the remaining oil in a large skillet. Pan-fry the potato patties, three or four at a time, for 6 to 8 minutes, turning midway, until golden brown.

Coconut-Cashew-Raisin Potato Patties

Makes 15 to 20 patties

Here is another variation of these tasty patties. Serve them with Tamarind Chutney (adding in dates) (page 119).

4 medium-size potatoes, boiled, peeled, and mashed	1 teaspoon sesame seeds
2 cups all-purpose flour	1 teaspoon sugar
1 tablespoon powdered coconut	6 to 9 cashew nuts, finely ground
1$^1/_2$ teaspoons finely grated ginger	10 to 12 raisins, finely chopped
$^1/_2$ teaspoon finely minced green chili pepper	1 cup finely chopped fresh cilantro
1 teaspoon *garam masala*	Juice of 1 lemon
	$^1/_2$ cup oil

Divide the mashed potatoes into 2 equal portions. Combine the first portion with 1 cup of the flour. Combine the second portion with the coconut, ginger, green chili, *garam masala*, sesame seeds, sugar, cashews, raisins, cilantro, and lemon juice. Mix thoroughly.

With the potato-flour mixture, make fifteen to twenty small balls. Flatten each ball with your hand or a rolling pin to make a patty. Place 1 tablespoon of the other potato mixture on each patty. Pull the edges of the patty around the "stuffing" to form a 1- to 2-inch ball. Oil your hands and flatten each ball into a 2- to 3-inch patty with your palm.

Heat the oil in a skillet over medium heat. Coat each patty with the remaining flour, shake off the excess, and pan-fry for 1 to 2 minutes on each side, or until golden brown.

Zesty Potatoes

These simple, flavorful potatoes are easy to prepare for a snack or light meal. They are perfect served with any flatbread, but would be particularly good with Puris (page 50). They can be served hot or cold.

3/4 cup chickpea flour (besan)	1 teaspoon salt
1/2 teaspoon ground cayenne pepper	2 tablespoons oil
1/2 teaspoon *garam masala*	1 pound medium-size potatoes, boiled,
1/2 teaspoon ground cumin	peeled, and cut into 1/8-inch slices

 Combine the chickpea flour, cayenne, *garam masala*, cumin, and salt in a bowl. Mix thoroughly.

In a medium-size skillet, heat the oil over medium heat. Add the flour mixture and sauté for 30 seconds. Add the potato slices and mix well. Reduce the heat to medium-low and continue to cook for 10 to 15 minutes, or until the potatoes are cooked through.

Potatoes and Flaked Rice

Potato Pawa

Flaked rice, which has been pressed and flattened, is available at Indian grocery stores. This spicy snack mix combines the sweetness of sugar and coconut, with the fire of chili peppers.

5 cups flaked rice (pawa)	$1/2$ to 1 teaspoon finely chopped green chili pepper
2 tablespoons oil	Juice of 1 lemon
1 teaspoon black mustard seeds	1 teaspoon sugar
$1/4$ teaspoon asafoetida powder	$1/2$ teaspoon turmeric
1 pound potatoes, peeled and chopped into bite-size pieces	1 teaspoon salt
2 medium onions, chopped fine	2 tablespoons grated coconut
$1^1/2$ teaspoons finely grated fresh ginger	$1/4$ cup finely chopped fresh cilantro

 Wash the flaked rice in two or three changes of water. Drain and set aside.

Heat the oil in a large pan or skillet over medium heat. Add the mustard seeds and asafoetida powder. Sauté for 30 seconds or so, until the seeds crackle and are browned. Add the potato, stir well, and continue to cook until the potatoes are cooked through.

Add the onions and sauté for 1 to 2 minutes, until softened. Add the ginger, chili pepper, lemon juice, and sugar. Stir well.

Add the flaked rice, turmeric, and salt. Stir well and continue to cook for 2 to 3 minutes, until the mixture is heated through. Top with the coconut and cilantro before serving.

Cabbage Fritters

Cabbage Gota

The shredded cabbage in these tasty fritters gives them a soft texture and unique flavor. They are a perfect party appetizer or afternoon snack. Serve them with Cilantro Chutney (page 118) on the side.

1 head cabbage, finely shredded	$^1/_2$ teaspoon peppercorns, crushed (optional)
2 green onions, finely chopped	1 teaspoon salt
$^1/_2$ to 1 green chili pepper, finely chopped	$^1/_4$ cup finely chopped fresh cilantro
1 tablespoon garlic-ginger paste	$^1/_2$ cup all-purpose flour
$^1/_2$ teaspoon ground cayenne pepper	1 cup chickpea flour *(besan)*
$^1/_2$ teaspoon turmeric	$^1/_2$ cup uncooked Cream of Wheat
$^1/_2$ teaspoon ground cumin	$^1/_4$ cup plain yogurt
$^1/_2$ teaspoon ground coriander	1 teaspoon sugar
1 teaspoon fennel seeds	$^1/_2$ teaspoon baking soda
1 teaspoon coriander seeds, crushed	2 cups oil for deep-frying
$^1/_2$ teaspoon *garam masala*	

 In a large bowl, combine all the ingredients except the oil. Mix thoroughly and add $^1/_4$ to $^1/_2$ cup of warm water to make a thick batter. Set aside for 30 minutes.

Heat the oil in a *kadhai*, wok, or other pan appropriate for deep-frying over low-heat. Stir the batter thoroughly. When the oil is hot, drop in tablespoonfuls of the batter (you can fill one spoon with batter and use another to scrape it off into the oil) and fry for 30 seconds to 1 minute, turning midway, until golden brown. Drain the fritters on paper towels.

Kebab-Style Meatballs

These tasty little meatballs can be eaten plain or with a chutney. Coriander seeds are this recipe's secret ingredient and add an intense flavor. Use a mortar and pestle or a rolling pin to crush the seeds to release their flavor. Ground lamb is traditionally used in this dish, but ground beef can be substituted as well. You can include a green chili pepper for extra heat or substitute a bell pepper for a milder version.

---

1 large onion, very finely chopped

1 pound ground lamb or beef

1 green chili pepper, chopped fine, or $^1/_4$ cup finely chopped green bell pepper

$^1/_4$ cup finely chopped fresh cilantro

$^1/_4$ teaspoon ground cayenne pepper (or more according to taste)

$^1/_2$ teaspoon turmeric

$^1/_4$ to $^1/_2$ teaspoon *garam masala*

1 tablespoon coriander seeds, crushed

4 teaspoons garlic-ginger paste

$^3/_4$ teaspoon salt

1 egg, lightly beaten

1 teaspoon freshly squeezed lime or lemon juice

 Place the onion in cheesecloth in a colander placed in the sink, to drain the excess water for about 20 minutes. Squeeze out any remaining water with your hands and combine the onion with all the remaining ingredients. Mix well and form into fifteen to twenty small meatballs.

Heat oven to 350ºF. Place the balls on a baking sheet and bake for 20 minutes. Remove the tray from oven and turn the meatballs to ensure even cooking. Bake for an additional 20 minutes, or until the balls are browned. (Alternatively, you can deep-fry the meatballs in 1 cup of oil.)

Cocktail-Size Meat Samosas

Makes 30 samosas

Samosas are a snack favorite around the world these days and no Indian cookbook would be complete without a recipe for meat samosas. This one uses egg roll wrappers to save on time. The result is a crispy, savory treat that is perfect to serve at parties with any kind of chutney.

1 pound ground lamb or beef	1 teaspoon salt
2 tablespoons oil	Juice of $^1/_2$ lemon
2 large onions, finely chopped	1 to 2 green chili peppers, finely
3 tablespoons garlic-ginger paste	chopped
$^1/_2$ teaspoon ground cayenne pepper	$^1/_2$ cup chopped fresh cilantro
$^1/_2$ teaspoon turmeric	2 tablespoons chopped fresh mint
$^1/_2$ teaspoon ground cumin	10 egg roll wrappers
$^1/_4$ teaspoon ground coriander	2 cups oil for deep-frying
$^1/_2$ teaspoon *garam masala*	

Brown the lamb until no longer pink and drain thoroughly. Use your hands to squeeze out the excess fat.

Heat 2 tablespoons of oil in a medium-size skillet over medium heat. Add the onions and sauté for 3 to 5 minutes, until lightly browned. Add the ginger-garlic paste, cayenne, turmeric, cumin, coriander, *garam masala*, and salt. Sauté for 2 minutes. Add the meat, lemon juice, and green chili. Reduce the heat to medium-low, stir, and cook for 5 minutes longer. Stir in the cilantro and mint, and remove from the heat.

Cut each egg roll wrapper into three equal strips. Place 1$^1/_2$ tablespoons of the meat mixture on the end of one strip. Fold that corner over the meat mixture to form a triangle. Continue to fold the rest of the strip to make a triangular dumpling. Tuck in any leftover pieces and seal the edges with a few drops of water, using your fingers. Close tightly. Continue until all the wrappers and filling are used up.

Heat the 2 cups of oil over medium-low heat in a deep frying pan or *kadhai*. Drop in the samosas, 3 or 4 at a time, and cook, turning halfway until golden brown, about 1 to 2 minutes. Drain on paper towels before serving.

Breads

Rotlis

Makes 15 to 20 rotlis

These traditional flatbreads are called *chapati* in Hindi and *rotli* in Gujarat. Simple and delicious, Gujarati cooks can prepare a pile of fresh, hot rotlis in a matter of minutes. They are served with tea and a little ghee for breakfast, or enjoyed with fresh vegetables, dals, and curries at lunch and dinnertime.

4 cups chapati flour	3 tablespoons oil
1 teaspoon salt	1 cup warm water

Place 3 cups of the chapati flour in a medium-size bowl. Add the salt and oil. Mixing with one hand, slowly add the warm water, a few tablespoons at a time to form a dough. Knead the dough until it comes together and does not stick to the side of the bowl (use a little additional oil if necessary).

Divide the dough into fifteen to twenty equal portions. Roll each into an oval patty about $1/2$ inch thick. Dip the patty into the remaining flour, shake off the excess, and place on your work surface. With a rolling pin, gently roll the dough into a circle about 5 inches in diameter. Rotate the dough while rolling to ensure an even thickness.

Heat a nonstick skillet over medium heat for 2 to 3 minutes. Place the rolled-out rotli in the skillet. After 15 seconds, flip it, and use a folded cloth to rotate it to ensure even cooking, about 15 to 20 seconds. Flip again and rotate the other side for 10 seconds or so. Set aside on a plate.

Continue to roll out and cook the *rotlis*, stacking them on a plate, covered, to keep them warm.

Note: Alternatively, you can use an electric mixer with a dough hook attachment to make the dough. Place the ingredients in a mixing bowl in this order: flour, salt, oil, and water. Follow the manufacturer's instructions.

You can also use a bread machine to prepare the dough. Place the ingredients in the machine in the following order: water, oil, salt, and flour. Follow the manufacturer's instructions.

Shobha Foi's Puris

Puris are puffy, deep-fried breads that are equally good eaten alone as a snack or used to scoop up savory vegetables, dals, or meat dishes. Warm and flaky, they are an enticing treat at any meal. This recipe from my aunt, Shobha Chitnis, makes delicious puris that are perfect for family meals as well as parties and other gatherings.

---

5 cups chapati flour	$1^3/4$ to 2 cups oil
1 teaspoon salt (or to taste)	2 cups warm water
1 teaspoon cumin seeds, lightly crushed	

Combine the chapati flour and salt in a large bowl. Add the cumin seeds and drizzle in $1/4$ cup of the oil. Mix well with your hands until most of the lumps disappear and the mixture resembles coarse meal.

Slowly add the warm water, $1/2$ cup at a time, while kneading the dough. Knead the dough thoroughly for several minutes. You can add a little additional oil at the end if the dough is sticky.

Pinch off $1^1/2$-inch pieces of dough and form them into small patties about $1/2$ inch thick by $1^1/2$ inches wide. With a rolling pin, roll out each patty until it is about $3^1/2$ inches in diameter.

Heat $1^1/2$ to 2 cups of the remaining oil in a *kadhai* (see page 25), wok, or deep pan. When the oil is hot, fry two or three puris at a time, turning once to ensure even cooking, until they are light brown. They will cook quickly—in 15 to 20 seconds.

Drain the puris in a bowl lined with paper towels. Serve hot.

Potato Parathas

Makes 10 to 12 *parathas*

These tasty *parathas* (stuffed flatbreads) have a spicy potato filling. They can accompany vegetable or meat dishes or work well as a light meal with salad and chutney on the side.

1 medium onion	1 teaspoon *garam masala*
2 medium-size potatoes, boiled, peeled, and mashed	Juice of $^1/_2$ lemon
1$^1/_2$ teaspoons grated fresh ginger	2 cups chapati flour, plus additional for sprinkling
$^1/_2$ teaspoon finely minced green chili pepper	1 teaspoon salt
4 tablespoons finely chopped fresh cilantro	3 tablespoons oil, plus additional for pan-frying
2 teaspoons sugar	

To prepare the potato filling, grate the onion and place it in a sieve or cheesecloth. Allow to stand 15 minutes and then squeeze any remaining water out of the onion. Combine the onion with the potatoes, ginger, chili pepper, cilantro, sugar, *garam masala*, and lemon juice. Mix well.

In a separate bowl, combine the chapati flour, salt, and oil. Mix well with your hands. Slowly add $^1/_4$ to $^1/_2$ cup of warm water, a little at a time, and knead into a smooth, firm dough.

Divide the dough into 10 to 12 small balls about 1 inch in diameter. Sprinkle your work surface with a little flour. Place one ball on the board and use a rolling pin to roll it out into a circle about 4 inches in diameter. Place about 1 tablespoon of potato filling in the center. Pull the edges of the dough into the center so that the filling is covered and press to seal the edges. Gently roll out the filled dough patty to about 4 to 6 inches in diameter, being careful to avoid tearing the dough. Repeat for remaining dough balls.

Heat 1/4 teaspoon or so of oil on a skillet or *tawa* over medium-low heat. Place the stuffed *paratha* in the skillet and use a cloth or spatula to rotate it so it cooks evenly, for about 30 seconds to 1 minute. Flip the *paratha* and rotate again until it is browned. Continue to oil the skillet and repeat for remaining *parathas*. Place the cooked *parathas* on a plate lined with paper towels to drain any excess oil, then stack them, covered, to keep warm.

Radish Parathas

Makes 6 *parathas*

These *parathas* are stuffed with grated radishes, giving them a moist, crunchy texture. White or daikon radishes are available seasonally at Asian grocery stores and some farmer's markets. They are larger than their red relatives and therefore easier to use for this recipe. These *parathas* are delicious served with plain yogurt that has been sprinkled with a little ground cumin.

---

1 pound white radishes (daikon), washed, peeled and grated

1 teaspoon salt

1 cup chapati flour

2 tablespoons oil plus additional for pan-frying

$^1/_4$ cup warm water

$^1/_4$ teaspoon cumin seeds

$^1/_8$ teaspoon asafoetida powder

$^1/_2$ teaspoon ground cayenne pepper

 Combine the grated radish with $^1/_2$ teaspoon of the salt in a sieve set over a bowl or the sink. Set aside for 15 minutes, drain, and then use your hands to squeeze out any remaining liquid.

In another bowl, combine the chapati flour, $^1/_2$ teaspoon of the salt, and 1 tablespoon of the oil and mix well with your hands. Slowly pour in $^1/_4$ cup of warm water and work into a firm, springy dough. Add an additional tablespoon or two of water if the dough is too dry or if it is sticky. Set the dough aside to rest for 15 minutes.

Heat the remaining 1 tablespoon oil in a medium-size skillet over medium heat and add the cumin seeds. When the seeds pop, add the asafoetida powder, grated radish, and cayenne pepper. Reduce the heat to low and cook, stirring occasionally, for 10 to 15 minutes. Cool.

Divide the dough into twelve small balls. With a rolling pin, roll out a ball into a circle about 4 inches in diameter. Spread 1 tablespoon of the radish mixture over the dough. Roll out a second ball of equal size and place it on top of the first piece. Seal the edges by pressing them lightly with your fingers. Gently glide the rolling pin over the top to even it and seal the *paratha*. Repeat this process with the remaining balls of the dough and radish mixture.

Heat a skillet or *tawa* over medium heat. Heat about 1/4 teaspoon of oil and add the stuffed paratha. Reduce the heat to low and rotate the *paratha* using a spatula or cloth. Flip it after about 30 seconds and cook on the other side. Continue to cook the remaining *parathas* over low heat. Stack them on a plate, covered, to keep them warm.

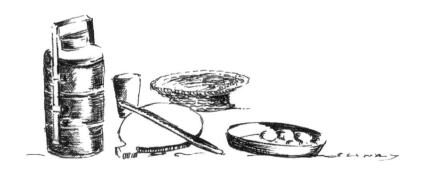

Rice Dishes

Plain Basmati Rice

Bhath

Basmati rice is so aromatic and flavorful that you need add little to it. Plain rice can be served with any vegetable, dal, or meat curry.

2 cups basmati rice	$^3/_4$ teaspoon salt
1 teaspoon ghee or butter	

Rinse the rice in 2 or 3 changes of water to release its starch.

Combine the rice, ghee, salt, and $3^1/_2$ cups of water in a medium-size pot. Bring to a boil and stir. Cover, reduce the heat to a simmer, and cook for 15 minutes, or until all the water is absorbed.

Seasoned Rice Pilaf

Bursting with colorful vegetables, aromatic cinnamon, cloves, and cardamom, this festive rice dish goes well with any meat or vegetable accompaniment. I find it easiest to use frozen mixed vegetables (the combination of peas, lima beans, corn, carrots, and green beans) but a similar combination of fresh diced vegetables works well too.

3 cups basmati rice	4 cardamom pods
2 teaspoons ghee	1 bay leaf
$1/2$ teaspoon peppercorns	$1/2$ cup diced frozen or fresh mixed vegetables
$1/4$ teaspoon whole cumin seeds	
$1/2$ teaspoon whole cloves	1 teaspoon salt
2 cinnamon sticks, broken into 1-inch pieces	$1/2$ teaspoon turmeric (optional)

 Rinse the rice in several changes of water to release its starch. Drain and place in a large pot with $4^1/2$ cups of water.

In a small pan, heat the ghee over medium heat. When it is hot, add the peppercorns, cumin seeds, cloves, cinnamon, cardamom, and bay leaf. Cook for 1 to 2 minutes, until the spices are brown and oil is seasoned.

Add the spice mixture to the rice, along with the mixed vegetables and salt. Add turmeric if desired (this gives the rice a festive yellow color). Stir well to combine. Cover and bring to a boil. Reduce the heat to low, stir, cover, and cook until the rice is done, about 20 minutes.

Rice with Lentils

Kitchdi

Makes six 1-cup servings

This is an evening meal staple at the Gujarati table, and most families enjoy *kitchdi* with a variety of different vegetables. It is traditionally eaten only with vegetable dishes.

$^1/_2$ cup masoor dal	$^3/_4$ teaspoon salt
2 cups basmati rice	1 teaspoon ghee or butter

Rinse the dal and rice in several changes of water to remove any impurities and release the starch. Drain and place in a medium-size saucepan. Add $3^1/_2$ cups of water, the salt and the *ghee* or butter. Stir to combine, cover, and cook over medium heat for 3 to 5 minutes, or until the water boils. Reduce the heat to very low and continue to cook, stirring occasionally, for 8 to 10 minutes, or until the rice is cooked.

Variation: You can also make *kitchdi* with *toor dal*. Since this dal takes longer to cook, soak it for several hours in warm water or, if you are short on time, cook it in enough water to cover for 10 to 15 minutes on the stove. Then proceed with the above recipe.

Seasoned Rice with Lentils

This slightly more complex version of rice with lentils gets its bright yellow color from turmeric, and an extra punch of flavor from black pepper.

3/4 cup *toor dal*	1/2 teaspoon turmeric
1 1/2 cups basmati rice	1/2 teaspoon black pepper
1 teaspoon salt	Tomato slices for garnish

 Soak the *toor dal* for 30 minutes in water to cover. Rinse the rice in two changes of water to release the starch and drain.

Combine the dal, rice, salt, turmeric, and black pepper in a medium-size pot. Add 3 cups of water and bring to a boil. Reduce the heat to a simmer, and cook, covered, for 15 to 20 minutes, until the rice is cooked. Garnish with tomato slices before serving.

Vegetables

Seasoned Chickpeas with Tomatoes

Channa Masala

Makes 4 to 6 servings

Chickpeas are a favorite in Indian cooking. They are inexpensive, easy to prepare and very nutritious. This recipe uses canned chickpeas to make the preparation very quick. It can be served with plain basmati rice or with any flatbreads. It is also delicious stuffed in pita bread, sandwich style.

---

2 teaspoons oil

1 small onion, chopped

$^1/_2$ cup chopped green bell pepper

1 large tomato, chopped

2 (14-ounce) cans chickpeas, drained and rinsed

2 tablespoons tomato paste

$^1/_4$ teaspoon salt (or to taste)

$^1/_4$ teaspoon ground cayenne pepper

$^1/_4$ teaspoon ground turmeric

$^1/_4$ teaspoon ground cumin

$^1/_4$ teaspoon ground coriander

$^1/_4$ teaspoon *garam masala*

1 teaspoon garlic-ginger paste

2 tablespoons chopped fresh cilantro

Heat the oil in medium-size pot over medium heat. Add the onion and bell pepper, and sauté until softened. Add the chopped tomato and continue to sauté until the tomatoes break down, forming a sauce. Reduce the heat slightly, and add the chickpeas and tomato paste, stirring to combine the ingredients. Add $^1/_4$ cup of water.

Add the salt, cayenne pepper, turmeric, cumin, coriander, *garam masala*, and garlic-ginger paste. Stir until the ingredients are well combined, adding more water if the mixture gets too dry.

Reduce the heat to low and simmer, covered, for 5 to 10 minutes. Top with fresh cilantro before serving.

Mashed Vegetables

Panv Bhaji   Makes 8 servings

The Gujarati name for this dish, *Panv Bhaji*, translates to "Vegetables with Bread."
Interestingly, these mashed vegetables are served on Western-style oven-baked bread
or buns, like a sandwich. They are also great served in pita bread. You can reduce the
amount of spices and serve these healthful mashed vegetables to toddlers or young
children. Prepared *Panv Bhaji masala* mix is available in Indian grocery stores.

---

1 head cauliflower, cut into small florets

2 medium-size potatoes, peeled and chopped into small cubes

1 medium-size eggplant, or 1/2 a large eggplant, trimmed and cut into 1-inch chunks

4 medium-size tomatoes, chopped

3 tablespoons oil

1/2 teaspoon black mustard seeds

2 large onions, finely chopped

1 tablespoon *Panv Bhaji masala*

1 teaspoon ground cayenne pepper

1/2 teaspoon turmeric

1/2 tablespoon ground cumin

1/2 tablespoon ground coriander

2 1/2 teaspoons salt (or to taste)

8 sandwich rolls

3/4 cup chopped fresh cilantro

1 to 2 green chilies, finely chopped

 Combine the cauliflower and potatoes with enough water to cover in a medium-size pot. Bring to a boil, reduce the heat to medium, and cook for about 15 minutes, until the vegetables are tender. In a separate pot, combine the eggplant and tomatoes. Cover with water, bring to a boil, reduce the heat to medium-low, and cook for 6 to 8 minutes. Drain all the vegetables, place in a large bowl, and mash into a chunky puree.

Heat the oil in a large pot over medium heat. Add the mustard seeds and cook for 1 to 2 minutes, until the seeds pop and turn brown. Add the onion (reserving 1/2 cup for topping) and sauté for 3 to 5 minutes, until light brown. Add the *Panv Bhaji masala*, cayenne pepper, turmeric, cumin, coriander, and salt. Mix well.

Add the mashed vegetables and sauté for about 5 minutes, until well mixed and heated through. Serve on sandwich rolls, topped with cilantro, green chili, and chopped onion.

Variation: Instead of serving the *Panv Bhaji* on buns, you can add one-half to one cup of water to the mashed vegetable mixture to make a hearty vegetable soup. Serve with crackers, bread, or flatbread on the side.

Sixth Day Mixed Vegetables

Chaati nu shaak

Makes 6 servings

This mixed vegetable combination is so named because it is typically served to new mothers six days after a baby is born. The vitamins and fiber in the vegetables are perfect postpartum foods, and the reduced amount of spices takes the breast-feeding mother into account. My mother made these vegetables for my sister and me after our children were born and we can certainly attest to its excellent taste and fortifying effects! Use as many different vegetables as you can for maximum flavor and nutrients, and serve with any rice or flatbread.

Use $1/4$ to $1/2$ cup of each of the vegetables you desire to make a total of about 2 pounds. Here are some suggestions:

Potatoes, peeled and cubed

Eggplant, trimmed and chopped

Okra, trimmed and chopped

Ghilora (tindora), trimmed and chopped

Bitter melon, peeled and chopped

Bottle gourd, chopped

Cauliflower florets

Cabbage, shredded

Carrots, chopped

Corn kernels

Green peas

Green beans, chopped

Pigeon peas

Spinach, steamed and chopped

Fenugreek leaves, chopped

Dill, chopped

3 to 4 tablespoons oil

$1/4$ teaspoon cumin seeds

$1/4$ teaspoon fenugreek seeds

$1/4$ teaspoon *ajwain* seeds

$1/4$ cup chopped onion

$1/4$ cup chopped bell pepper

$1/2$ teaspoon ground cayenne pepper

$1/2$ teaspoon turmeric

$1/2$ teaspoon ground cumin

$1/4$ teaspoon ground coriander

$1^1/2$ teaspoons salt

Heat the oil in a large skillet over medium-low heat. Add the cumin seeds, fenugreek seeds, and *ajwain* seeds. Sauté for 2 to 3 minutes, until the seeds are browned. Add the onion and bell pepper, and continue to sauté for 2 to 3 minutes. Add the cayenne, turmeric, cumin, coriander, and salt. Stir well and sauté for 30 seconds to release the flavors of the spices.

Add all the vegetables, EXCEPT any leafy greens. Reduce the heat to low, and cook, stirring for 5 to 10 minutes. Add any greens and cook until tender, about 10 more minutes.

Classic Gujarati Mixed Vegetables

Undhiyu

Makes 8 to 10 servings

This combination of root vegetables and beans is famed throughout India as the quintessentially Gujarati dish. It does require some preparation time, but the results are well worth the effort. It is wonderful served with Gujarati Yogurt Curry (page 93), any flatbread, and rice.

For the dumplings:

- 6 ounces fresh or frozen fenugreek leaves *(methi)* (about 1 cup chopped)
- 1/2 teaspoon salt
- 1/2 cup chickpea flour *(besan)*
- 2 tablespoons whole wheat flour
- 1/2 teaspoon ground cayenne pepper
- 1/2 teaspoon turmeric
- 1/4 teaspoon ground cumin
- 1/4 teaspoon ground coriander
- 1 tablespoon sugar
- 3 tablespoons oil plus 1/2 cup for frying

For the mixed vegetables:

- 6 tablespoons oil
- 2 medium-size potatoes, peeled and cut into 1-inch chunks
- 1 large sweet potato, peeled and cut into 1-inch chunks
- 2 large carrots, peeled and cut into 1-inch chunks

- 1 teaspoon salt
- 1 teaspoon *ajwain* seeds
- 1/4 teaspoon asafoetida powder
- 1 teaspoon *garam masala*
- 4 dried red chilies
- 1 to 2 green chilies, finely minced
- 2 teaspoons sesame seeds
- 1 1/2 tablespoons garlic-ginger paste
- 1/2 pound baby eggplants, trimmed and slit in half
- 1 small green bell pepper, chopped
- 1 pound *papdi (valor)* beans, strings removed
- 1 cup fresh or frozen *surti papdi lilva* (green kidney beans), parboiled
- 1 cup fresh or frozen *tuver lilva* (pigeon peas), blanched
- 1/2 cup unsweetened coconut flakes
- 3/4 cup chopped fresh cilantro

To prepare the dumplings, combine the fenugreek leaves with the salt in a colander set over a small bowl or the sink. Set aside for 15 minutes and then squeeze out any excess liquid with your hands. In the meantime, combine the chickpea flour, whole wheat flour, cayenne pepper, turmeric, cumin, coriander, sugar, and 3 tablespoons of the oil in a small bowl. Add the fenugreek leaves and combine thoroughly (use your hands if necessary) to form a thick dough. Add 1 to 2 tablespoons of water if necessary. Divide the dough into 12 to 15 small balls about $1/2$ inch in diameter. Heat $1/2$ cup of oil in a deep skillet or *kadhai*, and pan-fry the dumplings for 1 to 2 minutes, or until golden brown. Set aside.

For the vegetables: heat 3 tablespoons of the oil in a large pot over medium heat. Add the potatoes, sweet potatoes, carrots, and $1/2$ teaspoon of the salt. Sauté for 10 to 15 minutes, until the potatoes are softened. Transfer the potato mixture to a separate bowl.

Heat the remaining 3 tablespoons of oil in the pot. Add the *ajwain* seeds, asafoetida powder, *garam masala*, red chilies, green chilies, sesame seeds, garlic-ginger paste and the remaining $1/2$ teaspoon of salt. Sauté for 1 minute. Add the eggplant, bell pepper, *papdi* beans, *surti papdi lilva*, and *tuver lilva*. Stir well to coat the vegetables with the spices, and cook about 5 minutes. Add the potato-carrot mixture to the pot and stir well for another 5 to 10 minutes, or until the vegetables are cooked through. Combine the dumplings with the vegetables and top with coconut and cilantro before serving.

Eggplant and Potatoes

Ringan Bataka nu shaak

This is a flavorful eggplant dish that is dry (no sauce or curry)—that's why it is a perfect partner to Gujarati Yogurt Curry (page 93).

---

2 tablespoons oil

1/4 teaspoon mustard seeds

1 teaspoon garlic-ginger paste

2 medium-size Japanese eggplants, sliced into thin rounds

2 medium-size potatoes, peeled, cut in half lengthwise, and sliced thin

1/2 teaspoon ground cayenne pepper

1/4 teaspoon turmeric

1/2 teaspoon ground cumin

1/2 teaspoon ground coriander

1/2 teaspoon salt

 Heat the oil in a large skillet or sauté pan (a nonstick skillet works well) over medium heat. Add the mustard seeds, cover, and turn the stove off. When you hear the seeds crackle, remove the lid and add the garlic-ginger paste (stand a good distance from the pot as oil may splatter). Immediately add the eggplant and potatoes and stir to mix. Return the heat to medium-low.

Sprinkle the cayenne pepper, turmeric, cumin, coriander, and salt on top. Add 1 to 2 tablespoons of water and stir until the spices coat the eggplant and potatoes well.

Cover and cook, stirring every few minutes to prevent sticking, for about 15 minutes. Add more oil or water if the vegetables stick too much. The eggplant should be softened and the potatoes crispy and cooked through when they are done. Serve with Gujarati Yogurt Curry (page 93) and rice or your choice of bread.

Okra with Potatoes

Bhinda nu shaak

Makes 4 servings

This simple dish of crispy okra and potatoes is my childhood favorite. My mother always has it ready whenever I visit.

1/4 cup oil	3/4 teaspoon ground cayenne pepper
1/4 teaspoon cumin seeds	3/4 teaspoon turmeric
1 tablespoon garlic-ginger paste	1/2 teaspoon ground cumin
1 pound fresh okra, tops and bottoms trimmed, cut in half lengthwise, and then cut into thin strips lengthwise	1/2 teaspoon ground coriander
2 medium-size potatoes, peeled, cut in half lengthwise and sliced thin	1/2 teaspoon salt

---

Heat the oil in a large skillet or frying pan (nonstick works fine) over medium heat. Add the cumin seeds, cover carefully avoiding any sizzling oil that may fly out, and turn the stove off. Allow the seeds to crackle in the hot oil for 1 to 2 minutes.

Add the garlic-ginger paste to the pan and then the okra and potatoes. Return the heat to medium heat and stir until the okra is well coated. Reduce the heat to low, cover, and cook for 10 minutes or so, stirring occasionally to prevent sticking.

Sprinkle the cayenne pepper, turmeric, cumin, coriander, and salt over the vegetables. Mix well so that the okra is coated. Add a little additional oil or 1 tablespoon of water if the okra and potatoes begin to burn on the bottom.

Cover and cook over low heat for an additional 10 to 15 minutes, or until the potatoes are cooked through and the okra is crispy. If desired, remove the cover and increase the heat to medium during the last few minutes of cooking, to brown the okra and potatoes. Serve with Gujarati Yogurt Curry (page 93) and rice or *Chapatis* (page 49).

Stuffed Okra

Bharela Bhinda

Makes 4 servings

In this recipe, the okra are slit and stuffed with an enticing spice mixture. They make a lovely and tasty dinnertime presentation and are perfect served with Gujarati Yogurt Curry (page 93) or Rice with Lentils (page 59). Choose unblemished, firm, small- to medium-size okra for this dish.

1 pound okra	1 teaspoon salt
$^1/_2$ to $^3/_4$ teaspoon ground cayenne pepper	1 teaspoon ground peanuts
$^1/_2$ teaspoon ground cumin	$^1/_4$ teaspoon sesame seeds
$^1/_2$ teaspoon ground coriander	2 tablespoons oil
1 tablespoon grated fresh ginger	1 medium-size potato, peeled and julienned (optional)

 Wash and trim the tops and bottoms of the okra. Cut a slit along the length of each okra for the stuffing.

To prepare the stuffing, combine the cayenne, cumin, coriander, ginger, salt, peanuts, and sesame seeds in a small bowl.

Use a small spoon to fill each okra with $^1/_2$ teaspoon of the stuffing.

Heat the oil in a large skillet over medium heat. When the oil is hot, carefully place the okra in the skillet. Cover and cook for 5 minutes. Reduce the heat to low, and stir so that all sides of the okra are crisped, about 5 to 10 minutes. If desired, add the potatoes for the last 10 minutes or so of cooking. Stir well to coat the potatoes with the spices.

Cauliflower and Potatoes

Makes 4 to 6 servings

The combination of crisp cauliflower, tangy tomatoes, and nutritious *surti papdi lilva*, green kidney beans, (see page 20) in this dish make it a mealtime favorite in Gujarat. It stands on its own as a main dish when served with rice or any flatbreads. It is also a nice accompaniment to other vegetables or any meat curries.

1/4 cup oil	1 teaspoon salt
1 small onion, chopped	1 head cauliflower, cut into florets
3 teaspoons garlic-ginger paste	1 large potato, peeled and cut into
3 plum tomatoes, chopped	1-inch cubes
1 teaspoon ground cayenne pepper	1/2 cup frozen *surti papdi lilva* (green
1/2 teaspoon turmeric	kidney beans)
1 teaspoon ground cumin	1 green chili pepper (optional)
1 teaspoon ground coriander	3 tablespoons chopped fresh cilantro
1/2 teaspoon *garam masala*	

 Heat the oil in a large pot over medium heat. Add the onions and sauté until soft and light brown. Add the garlic-ginger paste and sauté for 1 minute. Add the tomatoes, cayenne pepper, turmeric, cumin, coriander, *garam masala*, and salt. Stir briskly and continue to cook for 1 to 2 minutes, until the tomatoes soften and a sauce begins to form. Add the cauliflower, potatoes, and 3/4 cup of water to the pot. Stir well, cover, and reduce the heat to a simmer.

Meanwhile, boil the *surti papdi lilva* in water for 5 to 7 minutes, until they are almost tender. Alternatively, you can microwave the beans by placing them in a microwave-safe bowl with 3/4 cup of water. Cover the bowl with a paper towel and microwave on HIGH for 3 minutes.

Trim the top of the green chili pepper and make a lengthwise slit in it (being careful not to cut it all the way apart). Add the chili pepper and *surti papdi lilva* to the cauliflower mixture. Continue to cook, covered, stirring occasionally for 15 to 20 minutes, until the potatoes are cooked through. Top with cilantro before serving.

Spinach with Potatoes and Eggplant

Palak ne Bhaji

Makes 4 to 6 servings

This is a perfect recipe for fresh, summertime spinach from the farmers' market. When paired with rice or chapatis, the spinach, potatoes, and eggplant make a hearty, vegetarian dish.

---

2 tablespoons oil

1/2 medium onion, chopped

1 teaspoon garlic-ginger paste

3/4 teaspoon ground cayenne pepper

1/2 teaspoon turmeric

1/2 teaspoon ground cumin

1/2 teaspoon ground coriander

1 teaspoon salt

2 small potatoes, peeled and cut into thin slices

1 medium-size eggplant, trimmed and sliced

1 pound fresh spinach, washed and trimmed

1/2 cup *tuver lilva* (pigeon peas) (see page 21), cooked (optional)

Heat the oil in a large skillet over medium heat. Add the onions and sauté until brown, about 3 to 4 minutes. Reduce the heat to medium-low, and add the garlic-ginger paste, cayenne, turmeric, cumin, coriander, and salt. Stir-fry for 2 minutes.

Add the potatoes and eggplant. Stir to coat with the spices. Reduce the heat to low, cover, and cook for 10 minutes, stirring occasionally. Add the spinach and *tuver lilva*, if desired. Cook for 5 to 7 minutes, until the spinach is wilted and the potatoes are cooked through.

Eggplant, Potatoes, and Beans

Ringan Papdi

Makes 4 to 6 servings

Here is another delightful vegetable dish that features *surti papdi lilva* (see page 20). Combined with eggplant and potatoes, the beans lend wonderful flavor and texture to this dish. It can be served on its own with rice or breads, and is especially good when accompanied by Gujarati Yogurt Curry (see page 93).

$^1/_2$ cup frozen *surti papdi lilva* (green kidney beans) (can be increased to 1 cup if desired)

3 tablespoons oil

$^1/_2$ teaspoon *ajwain* seeds

2 medium-size potatoes, peeled and cut into 1-inch pieces

1 teaspoon garlic-ginger paste

$^1/_2$ teaspoon ground cayenne pepper

$^1/_2$ teaspoon ground cumin

$^1/_4$ teaspoon ground coriander

$^1/_2$ teaspoon salt

2 medium-size Japanese eggplants, trimmed and cut into 1-inch pieces

 Boil the *surti papdi lilva* in water for 5 to 7 minutes, until they are almost tender. Alternatively, place the beans in a microwave-safe bowl with $^3/_4$ cup water. Cover the bowl with a paper towel and microwave on HIGH for 3 minutes. If you choose to use 1 cup of beans, double the amount of water.

Heat the oil over low heat in a large skillet. When the oil is hot, add the *ajwain* seeds and cover, cooking 1 to 2 minutes, until the seeds darken slightly. Quickly lift the lid, add $^1/_2$ cup of the potatoes, and re-cover. Add the garlic-ginger paste, stir, and cover again to avoid splattering. Cook for 1 minute, and then add the cayenne pepper, cumin, coriander, and salt, stirring well. Add the remaining potatoes, the eggplant, and the beans. Stir well so that the vegetables are coated with the spices. Increase the heat to medium-low, and cook, covered, for 10 to 15 minutes, or until the potatoes are cooked through, stirring frequently to avoid burning.

Papdi Beans with Eggplant

Papdi nu shaak

The combination of soft eggplant and firm *surti papdi lilva* (green kidney) beans in this dish give it an appealing texture. Serve with rice or any flatbread.

3 tablespoons oil	$^1/_2$ teaspoon turmeric
$^3/_4$ teaspoon *ajwain* seeds	$^1/_2$ teaspoon ground cumin
4 teaspoons garlic-ginger paste	$^1/_2$ teaspoon ground coriander
1 medium-size Japanese eggplant, cut into $1^1/_2$-inch chunks	$^1/_2$ teaspoon salt
1 teaspoon ground cayenne pepper	$^1/_2$ pound *surti papdi lilva* (green kidney beans), blanched

 Heat the oil in a medium-size skillet over medium heat. When the oil is hot, add the *ajwain* seeds and cook for 1 to 2 minutes, until the seeds are browned. Add the garlic-ginger paste and eggplant. Stir and cook for 1 minute.

Add the cayenne pepper, turmeric, cumin, coriander, and salt. Stir well, reduce the heat to medium-low, cover and cook for 5 minutes. Add the *surti papdi lilva*, reduce the heat to low, and cook for 5 more minutes.

Eggplant Stuffed with Spices

Bharela Ringan

Makes 6 servings

This recipe calls for small or "baby" dark purple eggplants, found at many Indian and Asian grocery stores. Look for small, firm eggplants with fresh, green stems. The potatoes provide a crunchy contrast to the soft eggplants in this dish. Serve with Rice with Lentils (page 59) and Gujarati Yogurt Curry (page 93).

2 tablespoons grated fresh ginger	1 teaspoon finely chopped green chili
1 teaspoon sesame seeds	1 teaspoon fennel seeds
1 teaspoon ground cayenne pepper	1 teaspoon oil, plus $1/2$ cup oil for frying
1 teaspoon turmeric	2 tablespoons chickpea flour (besan)
$1/2$ teaspoon ground cumin	$1^1/2$ pounds baby eggplant, washed and stems trimmed
$1/2$ teaspoon ground coriander	1 large potato, peeled and sliced into thin rounds
1 teaspoon salt	

To prepare the stuffing, combine the ginger, sesame seeds, cayenne pepper, turmeric, cumin, coriander, salt, green chili, and fennel seeds in a small bowl. Heat 1 teaspoon of oil in a small skillet over medium heat. Add the chickpea flour and cook, stirring constantly, for 1 to 2 minutes, until the chickpea flour is lightly browned. Combine the chickpea flour with the spice mixture and set aside to cool.

To prepare the eggplants for stuffing, make an incision to halve each eggplant, but be careful not to cut all the way through! Next, make smaller incisions (perpendicular to the large incision) to divide the eggplant into 6 to 8 pieces. Repeat for the remaining eggplants.

Using a small spoon or your fingers, fill the incisions in each eggplant with the stuffing mixture. You should use about 1 teaspoon of stuffing per eggplant.

Heat the remaining $1/2$ cup oil in a large skillet. When the oil is hot, add the stuffed eggplants and cover quickly to avoid splattering. Cook for 1 to 2 minutes. Turn the eggplants carefully to avoid breaking them. Move the eggplants toward the center of the skillet and place the potatoes around them along the edge of the pan.

Reduce the heat to low, cover, and cook for 20 to 25 minutes, turning the potatoes and eggplants every 5 minutes or so. Remove from heat when the eggplants are browned and crispy on the outside and the potatoes are cooked through.

Eggplant, Potato, and Tomato Curry

Ringan, Bataka, Tameta nu shaak   Makes 4 to 6 servings

This dish combines inexpensive and widely available vegetables in a fragrant, spicy sauce. Instead of grating the fresh ginger and finely chopping the green chili, you can combine the two in a blender and make a paste. Use one tablespoon of the paste for this recipe and save the remainder to add flavor to other dishes.

---

2 tablespoons oil

1/4 teaspoon cumin seeds

1/4 teaspoon black mustard seeds

1/4 teaspoon asafoetida powder

1 1/2 teaspoons finely grated ginger

1 1/2 teaspoons finely chopped green chili

2 small tomatoes, chopped

1 teaspoon ground cayenne pepper

1/2 teaspoon turmeric

1 teaspoon ground cumin

1/2 teaspoon ground coriander

1 teaspoon salt

1 green chili pepper, halved (optional)

1 cup *tuver lilva* (pigeon peas) (see page 21), blanched

2 medium-size potatoes, peeled and chopped into 1-inch chunks

1 medium-size Japanese eggplant, quartered lengthwise and cut into 1-inch chunks

2 tablespoons chopped fresh cilantro

 Heat the oil in a medium-size pot over medium heat. When the oil is hot, add the cumin seeds, mustard seeds, asafoetida powder, grated ginger, and finely chopped green chili. Sauté for 30 seconds and reduce the heat to medium-low. Add the tomatoes and stir well. Cover and cook for about 10 minutes, until the tomatoes are reduced to a sauce.

Add the cayenne pepper, turmeric, cumin, coriander, salt, and green chili. Mix well for about 1 minute, until the sauce becomes cohesive. Add the *tuver lilva*, potatoes, and eggplant. Stir well to coat the vegetables with the spices. Add 1/2 cup of water, cover, reduce the heat to a simmer, and cook for 10 minutes, or until the potatoes are cooked through. Garnish with cilantro before serving.

Ghilora and Potatoes

Makes 4 servings

Ghilora, also known as *tindora*, are a unique Indian vegetable and a favorite in Gujarat. You will find them in Indian grocery stores. They look like tiny green squashes (about two inches long and half an inch wide each). Choose the thinnest ones, as they will be easier to cut into small pieces. *Ghilora* can be enjoyed with rice and Gujarati Yogurt Curry (page 93) for dinner or with fresh Chapatis (page 49) for lunch.

$^1/_4$ cup oil	1 teaspoon ground cayenne pepper
$^1/_2$ teaspoon cumin seeds	1 teaspoon turmeric
$^1/_4$ teaspoon *ajwain* seeds	$^1/_2$ teaspoon ground cumin
4 teaspoons garlic-ginger paste	$^3/_4$ teaspoon ground coriander
$^3/_4$ pound fresh *ghilora*, tops trimmed and cut lengthwise into quarters	$^1/_2$ teaspoon salt
1 large potato, cut in half lengthwise and thinly sliced	

Heat the oil in a large skillet over medium heat. When the oil is hot, add the cumin seeds and *ajwain* seeds, covering immediately to prevent hot oil from splattering. Reduce the heat to low and allow the seeds to crackle for about 1 minute, or until they turn brown.

Add the garlic-ginger paste to the pan and then the *ghilora* and potatoes. Raise the heat to medium and stir well for about 5 minutes. Reduce the heat to low, cover, and cook for about 10 minutes, stirring occasionally to prevent sticking.

When the vegetables are light brown, add the cayenne pepper, turmeric, cumin, coriander, and salt. Mix well to coat the vegetables in the spices.

Cover and cook over medium-low heat for an additional 5 to 10 minutes, or until the potatoes and *ghilora* are cooked through and crispy. You can remove the cover during the last few minutes and allow some of them to brown to a darker crisp as this lends a nice crunchy texture to the dish.

Indian-Style Green Beans with Eggplant

Chora nu shaak   Makes 4 to 6 servings

Indian-style green beans are known as *chora*. They are almost a foot long and thinner than traditional green beans. You can find them in Indian groceries and Asian markets. This dish is particularly delicious enjoyed with fresh, hot *Chapatis* (page 49).

3 tablespoons oil	1 teaspoon salt
1/2 teaspoon whole cumin seeds	1 medium-size potato, peeled, halved lengthwise and thinly sliced
1/2 teaspoon *ajwain* seeds	1/2 pound Indian-style green beans *(chora)*, ends trimmed and cut into 1/2-inch pieces
1/4 teaspoon ground asafoetida	
1 1/2 teaspoons garlic-ginger paste	
1 teaspoon ground cayenne pepper	1 Japanese eggplant, trimmed and cut into 1-inch cubes
1/2 teaspoon turmeric	
3/4 teaspoon ground coriander	1 green chili pepper, trimmed, with an incision made in it lengthwise
1/2 teaspoon ground cumin	

 Heat the oil in a medium-size saucepan over medium-low heat. When the oil is hot, add the cumin seeds and *ajwain* seeds. Stir, cover, and allow to brown for 1 to 2 minutes. Add the asafoetida powder and garlic-ginger paste. Add the cayenne pepper, turmeric, coriander, cumin, salt, and potatoes, stirring to coat well. Cook, covered, for 5 minutes, stirring occasionally.

Add the *chora* and eggplant, and continue to stir. Add 1/2 cup of water and the green chili. Stir well, cover, and cook for 10 to 15 minutes, until the vegetables have softened and the potatoes are cooked through.

Indian-Style Green Beans

Chora nu shaak II

This is another method of cooking *chora* given to me by my mother's friend, Indu Makwana. Indu Auntie's recipe calls for tomatoes instead of eggplant. They add a zesty flavor to the *chora* and potatoes.

---

2 tablespoons oil

$1/2$ teaspoon *ajwain* seeds

$1/2$ dry red chili

1 medium-size tomato, chopped

1 tablespoon garlic-ginger paste

2 medium-size potatoes, peeled and julienned

1 teaspoon ground cayenne pepper

$1/2$ teaspoon ground coriander

$1/2$ teaspoon ground cumin

$1/2$ teaspoon salt

$1/2$ pound *chora* (Indian-style long green beans), ends trimmed and cut into $1/2$-inch pieces

$1/8$ teaspoon garam masala

Juice of $1/2$ lime

 Heat the oil over medium heat in a medium-size skillet. Add the *ajwain* seeds and cook for 2 minutes, or until the seeds are browned. Add the red chili, tomatoes, garlic-ginger paste, and potatoes. Stir, cover, and cook for 3 to 5 minutes.

Add the cayenne pepper, coriander, cumin, salt, and *chora*. Stir and cook for 5 minutes. Add the *garam masala* and lime juice. Stir, cover, and cook for 5 minutes, or until the potatoes are cooked through.

Sizzling Green Mango

Kachi Keri nu shaak

Makes 4 servings

Mangoes are not just for dessert! Here is a way to cook unripe, or green, mangoes. This spicy side-dish can be served with any flatbreads or over rice. Enjoy!

1 pound unripe mangoes	1/2 teaspoon ground cayenne pepper
2 tablespoons oil	1 teaspoon turmeric
1 teaspoon fenugreek seeds	1/2 teaspoon ground cumin
1 teaspoon black mustard seeds	1/4 teaspoon ground coriander
1/4 teaspoon asafoetida powder	1/2 teaspoon *garam masala*
2 dried red chili peppers	1 teaspoon salt
1 teaspoon crushed garlic	1 tablespoon sugar

 Wash, peel, and cut the flesh of the mango into chunks.

Heat the oil in a skillet over medium heat. Add the fenugreek seeds, mustard seeds, asafoetida powder, and chili peppers. Stir well for 1 minute. Add the mango and garlic. Cook and stirring for 5 to 10 minutes.

Reduce the heat to medium-low and add the cayenne, turmeric, cumin, coriander, *garam masala*, and salt. Stir well and cook for 10 to 15 minutes, until the mango is cooked through. Add the sugar, mix well, and remove from heat.

Spicy Fenugreek Leaves

Methi nu shaak   Makes 4 to 6 servings

Fenugreek leaves have a distinct, curry-like aroma and are available fresh, frozen or dried at Indian grocery stores. Use fresh or frozen leaves for this recipe. Serve with rice or flatbreads.

---

5 tablespoons oil

$^1/_2$ teaspoon whole cumin seeds

1 dried red chili, cut in half

1 small onion, chopped

1 large potato, peeled and cut into bite-size pieces

1 teaspoon garlic-ginger paste

1 teaspoon ground cayenne pepper

$^1/_2$ teaspoon turmeric

$^1/_2$ teaspoon ground cumin

$^1/_2$ teaspoon ground coriander

$^3/_4$ teaspoon salt

1 pound fresh or frozen fenugreek leaves *(methi)*, chopped (about 1$^1/_2$ cups)

1 medium-size eggplant, trimmed and cut into 1-inch pieces

$^1/_2$ green bell pepper, seeded and chopped

 Heat the oil in a large skillet over medium heat. Add the cumin seeds and red chili, and brown for 1 to 2 minutes. Add the onions and sauté for 5 minutes, or until soft. Add the potatoes and garlic-ginger paste, stirring well to coat. Sauté for an additional 5 minutes.

Add the cayenne pepper, turmeric, cumin, coriander, and salt. Stir well to coat. Add the fenugreek leaves, eggplant, and bell pepper. Stir well, reduce heat to low, and cover. Cook for 15 to 20 minutes, stirring occasionally to prevent burning, until the potatoes are cooked through.

Stuffed Chili Peppers

Tharela Marcha

Makes 8 servings

Adding spices to the already fiery green chili pepper makes for a very hot result! Enjoy these peppers as an accompaniment (like a spicy condiment) to a meal of vegetables and rice. You may want to keep some yogurt on hand to cool things down.

$^1/_4$ teaspoon ground cumin	1 teaspoon oil
$^1/_4$ teaspoon fennel seeds, crushed	8 small green chili peppers, ends trimmed
$^1/_4$ teaspoon *ajwain* seeds	
$^1/_4$ teaspoon salt	

 Combine the cumin, fennel seeds, *ajwain* seeds, and salt in a small bowl.

Make a lengthwise incision in each pepper for the stuffing. Distribute the spice mixture evenly into each incision.

Heat the oil in a small skillet over medium-low heat. When it is hot, Place the stuffed peppers in the skillet. Reduce the heat to low and cook for 15 minutes, turning occasionally to make sure the peppers are browned on all sides.

Stuffed Banana Peppers

Makes 5 servings

Banana peppers stuffed with spices are a tamer alternative to the previous recipe. Enjoy these served alongside rice and vegetables. Cut off bits of the pepper and mix it in with the other food on your plate to add flavor.

2^1/$_2$ teaspoons oil	^{1}/$_2$ teaspoon *ajwain* seeds, ground
^{1}/$_2$ medium onion, finely chopped (^{1}/$_4$ cup)	1 teaspoon ground fenugreek
1 tablespoon chickpea flour *(besan)*	^{1}/$_2$ teaspoon salt
^{1}/$_2$ teaspoon ground cumin	1 teaspoon lemon juice
	5 green banana peppers

 To make the stuffing, heat 1^1/$_2$ teaspoons of the oil in a small pan over medium-low heat. Add the onion, chickpea flour, cumin, *ajwain* seeds, fenugreek, and salt. Sauté for 3 to 5 minutes, until the mixture is browned. Remove from the heat, cool, and add the lemon juice. Mix thoroughly.

Make an incision along the length of each pepper. Remove any seeds. Divide the stuffing equally among the peppers.

Heat the remaining 1 teaspoon of oil in a pan over medium heat. Add the peppers and pan-fry for 5 to 10 minutes, until browned. Turn the peppers during cooking so they cook evenly.

Cabbage, Potatoes, and Pigeon Peas

Makes 6 servings

This tasty combination of vegetables is nutritious and easy to prepare. Serve with rice or chapatis.

1/2 cup fresh or frozen *tuver lilva* (green pigeon peas)	1 teaspoon turmeric
1/4 cup oil	1 teaspoon ground coriander
1 teaspoon cumin seeds	1/2 teaspoon ground cumin
4 teaspoons garlic-ginger paste	1/2 teaspoon *garam masala*
1 medium head cabbage, finely shredded	1 teaspoon salt
1 1/2 teaspoons cayenne pepper	1 medium-size potato, peeled and cut into 1-inch pieces

 Place the pigeon peas in a small pan and add enough water to cover by 2 inches. Cover and cook over medium heat until the peas are cooked, about 15 minutes. Drain and set aside. (Alternatively, place the peas in a microwave-safe dish with water, cover loosely, and microwave on HIGH for 5 to 7 minutes, until tender.)

Heat the oil in a large skillet over medium heat. Add the cumin seeds and brown for 1 minute. Add the garlic-ginger paste and stir quickly. Add a handful of shredded cabbage. The garlic-ginger paste coats the cabbage and the water from the cabbage keeps the mixture from burning. Add the cayenne pepper, turmeric, coriander, cumin, *garam masala*, and salt and stir well.

Add the remaining cabbage and potatoes. Stir and cook for 1 to 2 minutes. Add the pigeon peas. Reduce the heat to medium-low and cover. Cook, stirring frequently, for 20 minutes, or until the potatoes are tender. Add 1 tablespoon of water if the mixture becomes too dry.

Crispy Bitter Gourd

Karela

Makes 4 servings

Karela, or "bitter gourd" as it is referred to in Asian markets in the U.S., can be an acquired taste. The vegetable resembles a long, green, thorny squash and contains many seeds. Its signature bitter flavor makes a tasty, interesting dish.

3/4 pound *karela* (bitter gourd)	1 1/2 teaspoons garlic-ginger paste
2 teaspoons salt	1/2 teaspoon ground cayenne pepper
1/4 cup oil	1/2 teaspoon turmeric
1 teaspoon cumin seeds	1/2 teaspoon ground coriander
1 medium onion, chopped	1/2 teaspoon ground cumin

 Remove the bumpy skin from the *karela* with a knife or vegetable peeler. Slice the *karela* into very thin, round pieces. Place in a small bowl, sprinkle with salt, and set aside for 30 minutes.

Squeeze out the excess water from the *karela* with your hands.

Heat the oil in a medium-size skillet over medium heat. Add the cumin seeds and sauté for 1 minute, until brown. Add the onions and sauté for 5 minutes, until soft. Add the garlic-ginger paste, cayenne pepper, turmeric, coriander, and cumin, and stir well. Add *karela* and stir. Taste for salt at this point and add more if necessary. Reduce the heat to medium-low, cover, and cook for 15 minutes, stirring occasionally until the *karela* are crispy and browned.

Guvar Beans with Tomatoes

Guvar nu shaak

Makes 4 servings

Guvar beans resemble snap peas and are available in most Indian grocery stores. This vegetable dish is excellent served with hot basmati rice.

2 tablespoons oil	$1/2$ teaspoon ground coriander
$1/2$ teaspoon *ajwain* seeds	$1/2$ teaspoon ground cumin
1 tablespoon garlic-ginger paste	$1/2$ teaspoon salt
1 medium onion, cut in half and sliced	1 plum tomato, chopped
1 teaspoon ground cayenne pepper	1 teaspoon finely chopped green chili
1 teaspoon turmeric	$3/4$ pound *guvar*, ends trimmed

 Heat the oil in a medium-size skillet over medium heat. Add the *ajwain* seeds and cook for 1 to 2 minutes, until brown. Add the garlic-ginger paste and onion. Stir-fry for 5 minutes, until the onion softens. Add the cayenne pepper, turmeric, coriander, cumin, salt, and tomatoes. Stir and cook for 1 to 2 minutes, until the spices are well blended.

Add the green chili and *guvar*. Stir, cover, and reduce the heat to medium-low. Cook for 5 to 10 minutes, until the beans are soft and cooked through.

Turia Squash and Potatoes

Turia nu shaak   Makes 4 servings

Turia (also known as rough okra, ridged gourd, or silk squash) is a squash that is about eight to twelve inches long, with an off-white, mild flesh. In this recipe, the soft, spongy *turia* nicely absorbs the flavors of the spices.

1 pound *turia*, peeled and cut into 1-inch pieces	1/4 teaspoon ground coriander
2 tablespoons oil	1/2 teaspoon salt
1/4 teaspoon fenugreek seeds	1 teaspoon grated fresh ginger
1/4 teaspoon cumin seeds	1 plum tomato, chopped
1/4 teaspoon asafoetida powder	1 teaspoon finely chopped fresh green chili
1/2 teaspoon ground cayenne pepper	1 medium-size potato, peeled and cut into 1-inch chunks
1/2 teaspoon turmeric	
1/4 teaspoon ground cumin	

 Place the *turia* with enough water to cover in a pan and bring to a boil. Reduce the heat, cover and cook for 10 to 15 minutes. Alternatively, place the *turia* in a microwave-safe dish with water to cover. Microwave on HIGH for 5 minutes.

Heat the oil in a medium-size skillet over medium heat. When the oil is hot, add the fenugreek seeds and cumin seeds. Cook for 1 to 2 minutes, until the seeds are browned.

Add the asafoetida powder, cayenne pepper, turmeric, cumin, coriander, salt, and ginger. Add the tomatoes and green chili. Stir and cook for 1 to 2 minutes, until the tomatoes soften and a sauce begins to form.

Add the *turia* and potatoes. Mix well and cook over medium heat for 1 minute. Reduce the heat to a simmer, cover, and cook for 10 to 15 minutes, or until the potatoes are done. Add 1 to 2 tablespoons of water if necessary to prevent sticking.

Dals and Kadhis

Mung Beans

Mung Dal

Mung dal are mung beans. They add a strong, earthy flavor to this thick, creamy dal. This dal can be enjoyed poured over hot basmati rice or with chapatis. Tear the chapatis into small pieces and ladle the hot dal over them.

1 cup *mung dal*	1 teaspoon turmeric
3 tablespoons oil	1 teaspoon ground cumin
1 teaspoon cumin seeds	1 teaspoon ground coriander
1 medium onion, chopped	1 teaspoon salt (or more, if desired)
2 tablespoons garlic-ginger paste	1/2 medium green pepper, chopped
1 to 2 teaspoons ground cayenne pepper, as desired	Juice of 1/2 lime
	1/4 cup chopped fresh cilantro

 Place the dal in a medium-size bowl and add enough water to cover by 1 inch. Set aside and soak for 2 to 3 hours.

Heat the oil in medium-size pot over medium heat. Add the cumin seeds and sauté for 1 to 2 minutes, until browned. Add the onion and sauté for 5 minutes, or until soft. Add the garlic-ginger paste and stir well. Add the cayenne, turmeric, cumin, coriander, salt, and 1/2 cup of water. Stir well as a sauce forms, and add the green pepper. Sauté for 5 to 7 minutes.

When the water has evaporated and the spice mixture is paste-like, drain the dal and add it to the pot along with 4 cups of water. Stir well and bring to a boil. Reduce the heat to a simmer, cover, and cook for 45 minutes, stirring occasionally. The dal will soften and become thicker.

Add the lime juice, stir, cover, and cook for 5 additional minutes. Sprinkle with cilantro before serving.

Gujarati Dal

Toor dal (also spelled *tuver*) are yellow lentils. This is the most popular dal in Gujarat and in all of India, in fact. It can be served over plain, hot basmati rice, or with chapatis.

1 cup *toor dal* (yellow lentils)	1 teaspoon ground cayenne pepper
1/2 teaspoon baking powder	1/2 teaspoon turmeric
1 teaspoon salt	1 teaspoon ground coriander
2 tablespoons oil	1/2 teaspoon ground cumin
1/2 teaspoon black mustard seeds	1 teaspoon finely chopped fresh green chili
1/2 teaspoon fenugreek seeds	
1/2 teaspoon whole cumin seeds	1/2 teaspoon tamarind concentrate, dissolved in 2 tablespoons water
1 tablespoon garlic-ginger paste	
1/4 teaspoon asafoetida powder	3 tablespoons chopped fresh cilantro

 Rinse and drain the dal. Place in a large pot and add 3 cups of water, the baking powder, and the salt. Cover and bring to a boil. Reduce the heat to low and cook for about 1 hour, or until the dal is completely dissolved. Use a hand blender to make it completely smooth.

Heat the oil in a large pot over medium heat. Add the mustard seeds, fenugreek seeds, and cumin seeds. Cook for 1 to 2 minutes, until the seeds pop and begin to turn brown. Stir in the garlic-ginger paste.

Add the dal mixture and stir well. Add the asafoetida powder, cayenne pepper, turmeric, coriander, cumin, and green chili. Add more salt if desired and additional water if you prefer a thinner consistency.

Cover, bring to a boil, and cook for 5 minutes. Reduce the heat to low, cover, and cook for about 30 minutes, stirring occasionally. Add the tamarind during last 5 minutes of cooking and garnish with cilantro before serving.

Gujarati Yogurt Curry

Kadhi

This rich, creamy curry is another of my favorites from my mother's kitchen. It is a delicious, tangy accompaniment to many vegetable dishes, but some people enjoy Gujarati Yogurt Curry on its own simply sipped out of a bowl like soup.

---

1 tablespoon chickpea flour *(besan)*
1^1/$_2$ cups plain yogurt
^{1}/$_2$ teaspoon ground cayenne pepper
^{1}/$_2$ teaspoon turmeric
^{1}/$_2$ teaspoon ground cumin
^{1}/$_2$ teaspoon ground coriander
1 teaspoon *garam masala*
^{1}/$_2$ teaspoon salt

2 teaspoons ghee or butter
^{3}/$_4$ teaspoon whole cumin seeds
1 clove garlic, thinly sliced
8 to 10 dried curry leaves
1 small green chili pepper, with an incision made along its length
2 tablespoons chopped fresh cilantro

 In a medium-size bowl, combine the chickpea flour and 1 tablespoon of water until a smooth paste forms. Add the yogurt and stir until combined. Add 1^1/$_2$ cups of water, and the cayenne pepper, turmeric, cumin, coriander, *garam masala*, and salt to the yogurt mixture.

Heat 1 teaspoon of the ghee in a medium-size saucepan over medium-low heat. Add the cumin seeds and fry for about 30 seconds. Add the garlic and allow it to brown slightly.

Slowly add the yogurt mixture to the pan, being careful to avoid splattering. Stir continuously to prevent curdling.

Bring to a boil for 1 minute, stirring as the mixture thickens and rises in the saucepan, adding a little more water if it becomes too thick.

Reduce the heat to low, add the remaining 1 teaspoon of ghee, the curry leaves, and the chili pepper. Cook for another 1 to 2 minutes, stirring constantly. Garnish with chopped cilantro and serve hot with vegetable dishes and rice.

Hema Masi's Gujarati Kadhi

This is a "dressed up" version of Gujarati *Kadhi* from my aunt, Hema Parmar. You will find that every Gujarati cook has her own combination of ingredients for this staple. Hema Masi adds some extra ingredients like *gur*, garlic stalks, and fenugreek leaves to the basic recipe to give it a robust and appealing flavor. Garlic stalks are available in Indian grocery stoves, or you can grow them yourself by simply planting garlic bulbs and letting the green stalks grow. Serve this alongside dry vegetable dishes or potatoes, or you can serve it in small stainless-steel bowls to be sipped and enjoyed on its own.

2 cups yogurt	$1/2$ teaspoon ground coriander
$1/4$ cup chickpea flour *(besan)*	1 tablespoon garlic-ginger paste
2 tablespoons ghee or butter	2 teaspoons salt
1 teaspoon whole cumin seeds	1 teaspoon *gur* (optional)
1 teaspoon whole cloves	2 cloves garlic, chopped
Pinch of fenugreek seeds	4 to 6 fresh garlic stalks, chopped
4 dried red chilies	2 large green chilies, with an incision made along its length
1 tablespoon dry or fresh curry leaves	
1 teaspoon turmeric	$1/4$ cup dry fenugreek leaves (optional)
$1/2$ teaspoon ground cumin	$1/4$ cup chopped fresh cilantro

 Combine the yogurt, chickpea flour, and 2 cups of water in a medium-size bowl. Stir well with a spoon or whisk until smooth.

Heat the ghee in a large saucepan. Add the cumin seeds and cloves, stirring well. Add the fenugreek seeds, dried red chilies, and curry leaves, and continue to stir.

Add the yogurt mixture to the saucepan along with $1^1/2$ cups water. Stir immediately so that lumps do not form. Add the turmeric, cumin, coriander, garlic-ginger paste, salt, and *gur*, if desired. Stir continuously to combine the ingredients and avoid lumps. Add the garlic, garlic stalks, green chilies, and fenugreek leaves.

Reduce the heat to low and continue to cook for 10 to 15 minutes, stirring frequently. The *kadhi* will thicken slightly as it cooks. Top with cilantro before serving.

Meat, Poultry, and Fish

Mutton Curry

Makes 6 servings

Mutton curry is enjoyed in Gujarat by nonvegetarians like Muslims and Christians. Lamb or goat is the meat of choice, but beef can be substituted. This hearty curry is wonderful served with plain or seasoned basmati rice and *Raita* (page 117).

1/4 cup oil

2 medium onions, finely chopped

2 tablespoons garlic-ginger paste

5 to 10 whole black peppercorns

5 to 10 whole cloves

1/4 teaspoon cardamom seeds

1 teaspoon ground cayenne pepper

1 teaspoon ground cumin

1 teaspoon ground coriander

1 teaspoon *garam masala*

1 teaspoon salt

2 medium-size tomatoes, chopped

1 to 2 fresh green chilies, minced

2 pounds lamb or goat meat, trimmed of fat and cut into 1-inch chunks

2 tablespoons chopped fresh mint

 Heat the oil in a large pot over medium heat. Add the onions and sauté until lightly browned, about 5 minutes. Add the garlic-ginger paste, peppercorns, cloves, cardamom, cayenne, cumin, coriander, *garam masala*, and salt. Sauté for 2 to 3 minutes to release the flavors from the spices.

Add the tomatoes and green chilies. Stir well. Add the meat and stir to coat with the spices and tomatoes. Add 2 1/2 cups of water. Reduce the heat to medium-low, cover, and cook for about 30 minutes, until the meat is cooked and the sauce is thickened. Top with chopped mint before serving.

Parsi-Style Lentil and Meat Curry

Dhansak

Makes 12 to 15 servings

This is a traditional Parsi specialty that is enjoyed by many people across Gujarat. This recipe yields a large quantity and can be halved if desired. *Dhansak* is a festive, celebratory dish that is perfect for large gatherings (it was served at my wedding, in fact). It is delicious over a steaming plate of basmati rice. Note that the *toor dal* must be soaked for one hour before cooking begins.

$1^1/_2$ cups *toor dal* (yellow lentils)

2 pounds lamb or beef, cubed

1 pound green bottle gourd, peeled and chopped into 1-inch pieces

6 tablespoons oil

1 teaspoon whole cumin seeds

1 teaspoon fenugreek seeds

Heaping $^1/_4$ teaspoon asafoetida powder

2 large onions, chopped

2 tablespoons garlic-ginger paste

3 plum tomatoes, chopped

1 small green bell pepper, chopped

$^1/_2$ cup chopped fresh or frozen fenugreek leaves *(methi)*

3 tablespoons cider vinegar (or other sweet vinegar)

$1^1/_2$ teaspoons ground cayenne pepper

$1^1/_2$ teaspoons turmeric

1 teaspoon ground cumin

$1^1/_2$ teaspoons ground coriander

2 teaspoons *garam masala*

1 teaspoon sugar

2 green chilies, trimmed and cut into small pieces

$^1/_2$ cup chopped fresh mint

$^1/_2$ cup chopped fresh cilantro

Place the dal in a medium-size pot and add water to cover by at least 2 inches. Cover and set aside for 1 hour.

Drain the dal and rinse it several times. Return it to the pot. Add 3 cups of water to the pot and bring it to a boil. Cover, lower the heat to a simmer, and continue to cook until the lentils dissolve into a thick gravy, about 30 minutes. (Alternatively, you can use a pressure cooker to reduce the cooking time.)

Meanwhile, place the lamb with 4 cups of water in a separate pot. Bring to a boil, cover, and reduce the heat to a simmer. Cover and cook until the meat is cooked through, about 25 minutes. (Note: Cooking times vary for lamb and beef, so make sure the meat is cooked.)

Place the gourd pieces in a small pan and cover with water. Boil for 10 to 15 minutes, until almost cooked through. (Alternatively, you can put them in a microwave-safe dish with water, cover, and cook on HIGH for 4 to 5 minutes.)

In a separate large pot, heat the oil over medium-low heat. Add the cumin seeds and fenugreek seeds, and cover. When the seeds turn brown, after 1 to 2 minutes, add the asafoetida powder and the onions. Stir well and cook over medium heat for 5 to 10 minutes, until the onions are soft.

 Add the garlic-ginger paste and continue to stir and cook for about 10 minutes, until the onions are brown. Then add the tomatoes and bell pepper. Cover and continue to cook, stirring occasionally, until the tomatoes are soft and a sauce begins to form, about 5 to 10 minutes. Add the gourd pieces and the fenugreek leaves.

Add the vinegar, cayenne, turmeric, salt, cumin, coriander, *garam masala*, sugar and green chilies. Add about 2 cups of water (or to desired thickness). Bring to a boil, cover, and then simmer for about 10 minutes, stirring occasionally.

Top with fresh mint and cilantro before serving.

Ground Lamb Curry

Kheemo nu shaak

Makes 8 servings

The distinct flavor of lamb in combination with vegetables makes this a hearty favorite. Ground beef can be substituted for the lamb. Serve with hot chapatis.

1/2 cup oil	1 teaspoon salt
1 large onion, chopped	2 teaspoons ground coriander
1/2 medium green bell pepper, chopped	1 teaspoon ground cumin
	2 teaspoons *garam masala*
3/4 cup fresh or frozen *tuver lilva* (green pigeon peas)	2 large potatoes, cut into 1-inch chunks
	3 pounds ground lamb, browned and drained
2 tablespoons garlic-ginger paste	
4 medium-size tomatoes, chopped	1 teaspoon lime juice
1 1/2 teaspoons ground cayenne pepper	1/4 cup chopped fresh mint
1 teaspoon turmeric	1/4 cup chopped fresh cilantro

 Heat the oil in medium-size pot over medium heat. Add the onion and sauté for 5 to 10 minutes, until the onions are soft and light brown. Add the bell peppers and continue to sauté for 5 minutes.

Place the *tuver lilva* in a small pan and add enough water to cover by 2 inches. Cover and cook over medium heat until the peas are cooked, about 15 minutes. Drain and set aside. (Alternatively, place the peas in a microwave-safe dish with water, cover loosely, and microwave on HIGH for 5 to 7 minutes, until tender.)

Add the garlic-ginger paste and tomatoes to the onions. Sauté over medium-low heat until the tomatoes are soft and a sauce forms, about 5 to 10 minutes.

Add the cayenne, turmeric, salt, coriander, cumin, and *garam masala*. Stir well and continue to sauté for 5 minutes. Add the *tuver lilva*, potatoes, lamb, lime juice, and 2$^1/_2$ cups of water. Stir well to combine. Cover and cook over medium-low heat, stirring occasionally, until the potatoes are done, about 15 to 20 minutes.

Garnish with mint and cilantro before serving.

Chicken Curry

Murghi

When I was growing up, this versatile dish appeared on our table on a weekly basis. It is hearty and easy to whip up for a crowd, and my mother has become quite well known for her version (below). Sometimes I add a little yogurt or coconut milk to make a creamier curry. You can also forgo those additions and serve a little *Raita* (page 117) on the side. Either way, it is a tasty curry that has become a favorite among many of my friends now too.

---

1 tablespoon oil

1 small onion, chopped

$^1/_2$ medium green bell pepper, chopped

1 tablespoon garlic-ginger paste

$^1/_2$ teaspoon ground cayenne pepper

$^1/_2$ teaspoon turmeric

$^1/_2$ teaspoon ground cumin

$^1/_2$ teaspoon ground coriander

$^1/_2$ teaspoon *garam masala*

1 teaspoon salt

2 cups chopped ripe tomato, or 1 (14.5-ounce) can whole, peeled tomatoes, undrained and coarsely chopped

2 tablespoons tomato paste

1 pound chicken (skinless, boneless breast or thighs or a combination), cut into bite-size pieces

2 medium-size potatoes, peeled and cut into $1^1/_2$-inch chunks

$^1/_2$ cup yogurt (optional)

$^1/_4$ cup chopped fresh cilantro

 Heat the oil in large pot over medium heat. Add the onion and bell pepper, and sauté for 5 minutes, until softened. Add the garlic-ginger paste, cayenne, turmeric, cumin, coriander, *garam masala*, and salt. Stir the spices into the onion mixture and cook for 1 minute. Add the tomatoes, tomato paste, and $1^1/_2$ cups of water. Stir well.

Add the chicken and potatoes, stir well, and add enough water to cover. Cover and cook over medium heat, stirring occasionally, for about 20 minutes, or until the chicken and potatoes are cooked through.

If you would like to add yogurt, whisk it with $^1/_4$ cup of water until smooth and then add it to the curry, stirring constantly to avoid curdling. Sprinkle with fresh cilantro and serve with hot rice or Chapatis (page 49).

Parsi-Style Chicken Curry

Parsi Murghi

Makes 8 to 10 servings

This version of chicken curry includes Indian poppy seeds, which unlike the European variety, are beige in color (see page 19). Coconut milk also gives it a rich flavor and creamy consistency. Serve over hot rice.

$1/4$ cup oil

1 medium onion, peeled, chopped, and processed to a paste in blender

2 tablespoons garlic-ginger paste

1 teaspoon ground cayenne pepper

2 teaspoons ground cumin

1 teaspoon ground nutmeg

2 teaspoons poppy seeds

2 teaspoons finely chopped fresh cilantro

2 teaspoons salt

3 pounds boneless, skinless chicken, breasts or other parts, cut into chunks

1 large tomato, chopped

4 medium-size potatoes, peeled and cut into chunks

1 cup coconut milk

Heat the oil over medium heat in a large pot. Add the onion paste and sauté for 2 to 3 minutes, until it turns light brown. Add the garlic-ginger paste, cayenne, cumin, nutmeg, poppy seeds, and cilantro. Reduce the heat to medium-low and sauté for 3 minutes, until the mixture becomes reddish brown.

Add the salt and chicken, and sauté for 5 minutes. Add the tomatoes, potatoes, and $1^1/2$ cups of water. Reduce the heat to a simmer, cover, and cook for 30 minutes.

When the sauce has thickened and the chicken and potatoes are cooked, remove from the heat. Stir in the coconut milk just before serving.

Tandoori Chicken

Tandoor ovens date back to the Mughals (Muslims) who arrived in northern India in the sixteenth century. Today, these clay ovens are used to make chicken and meat dishes as well as fluffy naan flatbreads and other favorites of Mughal cuisine that are popular all over India. Although proper tandoori chicken requires a tandoor oven, this recipe improvises nicely with a grill or regular oven. While this is not a Gujarati specialty per se, it is widely enjoyed throughout Gujarat, so I've decided to include it here.

1 cup plain yogurt	1 teaspoon salt
2 tablespoons garlic-ginger paste	3 tablespoons tandoori paste (see page 21)
1/2 teaspoon ground cayenne pepper	3 pounds chicken parts, skin removed
2 teaspoons ground cumin	1 onion, sliced into rings
1 teaspoon ground coriander	2 lemons, sliced
1 teaspoon *garam masala*	

 To prepare the marinade, combine the yogurt, garlic-ginger paste, cayenne, cumin, coriander, *garam masala*, salt, and tandoori paste in a large bowl. Prick the chicken parts with a fork and add them to the marinade. Coat thoroughly, cover with plastic wrap, and marinate in the refrigerator for 4 to 6 hours.

Preheat the oven to 350ºF and grease a baking sheet. If grilling, prepare a hot charcoal fire until the coals are white or heat a gas grill. Place the chicken pieces on the grill and cook for about 10 minutes on each side, or until done. If baking, place the chicken pieces on the baking sheet. Bake for 15 minutes and then turn the pieces. Bake for 15 to 20 additional minutes, or until the chicken is cooked through. For a crispier result, place the chicken under the broiler for 2 minutes at the end. Serve with onion rings and lemon slices.

Spicy Baked Chicken

Makes 6 to 8 servings

My mother likes to use chicken drumsticks for this recipe and serve it at parties because they are easy to hold and eat, but you can use other chicken parts or even a whole chicken (see variation below). The chicken drumsticks can also be deep-fried but this recipe provides directions for the healthier alternative of baking it. While this recipe has been modified with some non-Indian ingredients like soy sauce and all-purpose flour, it is such a hit at our house that I decided to include it here anyway. Be sure to allow time for the chicken to marinate in the spices.

$^1/_2$ medium onion, quartered

1 tablespoon soy sauce

$1^1/_2$ tablespoons garlic-ginger paste

$^1/_2$ teaspoon ground cayenne pepper

$^1/_2$ teaspoon *garam masala*

2 pounds chicken drumsticks

$^1/_2$ cup all-purpose flour

 Place the onion in a blender or food processor, and process until a rough puree forms. Place the onion in cheesecloth and allow the excess water to drain for about 20 minutes. To prepare the marinade, combine the onion with the soy sauce, garlic-ginger paste, cayenne, and *garam masala*. Add the chicken drumsticks and marinate in the refrigerator for 4 to 24 hours.

Heat the oven to 350°F. Remove each drumstick from the marinade, coat with flour, and place on a baking tray. Bake for 30 to 40 minutes, turning the pieces about halfway through. For extra crispiness, place the chicken under the broiler for 2 minutes at the end of the cooking time.

Variation: This recipe can be modified to prepare a whole (5- to 6- pound) chicken as well. Prepare the marinade as instructed above. Cut a few slits in the breast and legs so that the spices will be thoroughly absorbed. Then coat the chicken well with the spice marinade. Bake at 350°F for 1 1/2 to 2 hours, or until a meat thermometer inserted in the meaty part of the thigh reads 180°F.

Chicken Rice Pulao

Makes 8 servings

This is an easy, hearty, one-dish chicken and rice meal. It's perfect for entertaining guests or taking to a potluck. You can add small frozen mixed vegetables along with the rice at the end to give it additional texture and color. This dish is also delicious served with *Raita* (page 117).

---

2 tablespoons ghee or butter
1 teaspoon whole cumin seeds
1 medium onion, finely chopped
4 to 5 bay leaves
2 sticks cinnamon
4 to 5 curry leaves
1 tablespoon garlic-ginger paste

$^1/_2$ teaspoon ground cayenne pepper
1 teaspoon turmeric
1 teaspoon *biryani masala* (see page 13)
1 teaspoon salt
2 boneless, skinless chicken breasts, cut into bite-size cubes
$2^1/_2$ cups basmati rice

Heat the ghee in a large pot over medium heat. Add the cumin seeds. When the seeds pop and begin to turn brown, add the onion, bay leaves, cinnamon, and curry leaves. Sauté for 3 to 5 minutes, or until the onions soften. Then add the garlic-ginger paste, cayenne pepper, turmeric, *biryani masala*, salt, and chicken. Stir well to coat the chicken with the spices, and cook for 5 to 10 minutes, until the chicken is cooked.

Reduce the heat to low and add the rice with $3^1/_2$ cups of water. Stir well, cover, and cook for 10 to 15 minutes, until the rice is tender.

Chicken Biryani

Murghi Biryani

Makes 12 servings

Biryani is the classic Indian meat and rice combination, and it is enjoyed widely in Gujarat. This version calls for chicken, but an equal amount of lamb or beef could be substituted. You can halve this recipe if desired, but biryani is usually prepared in large quantities for family gatherings or special occasions. Leftovers freeze well. Cool yogurt Raita (page 117) is a must alongside this spicy dish.

$^1/_4$ cup oil	6 bay leaves
2 large onions, sliced lengthwise	10 to 15 curry leaves
3 tablespoons garlic-ginger paste	3 pounds boneless, skinless chicken
3 tablespoons yogurt	breasts or other chicken parts, cut into chunks
1 (8-ounce) can tomato sauce	$3^1/_2$ cups basmati rice
2 medium-size tomatoes, chopped	$^1/_8$ teaspoon saffron strands
1 (2.62-ounce) package *biryani masala* mix (such as Shan's; see page 13), or less to taste	$^1/_2$ cup cashew nuts, coarsely chopped (optional)
1 teaspoon turmeric	$^1/_4$ cup raisins (optional)
2 teaspoons ground cumin	2 hard-boiled eggs, peeled and sliced (optional)
1 teaspoon ground coriander	$^1/_4$ cup chopped fresh cilantro
2 teaspoons salt	

 Heat the oil in a large pot over medium heat. Add the onions and fry until browned, about 5 to 10 minutes. Using a slotted spoon so that excess oil drains, remove half the onions and place them in a bowl lined with paper towels; set aside.

Meanwhile, add the garlic-ginger paste, yogurt, tomato sauce, tomatoes, *biryani masala* mix, turmeric, cumin, coriander, and 1 teaspoon of the salt to the onions that remain in the pot. Reduce the heat to low, stir well, and add the bay leaves, curry leaves, and chicken. Cover and cook on low heat, stirring frequently, for 30 minutes while you prepare the rice.

In a separate pot, combine the rice with the remaining 1 teaspoon of salt and 8 cups of water. Bring to a boil, cover, reduce the heat to a simmer, and cook for 20 minutes, or until the rice is done. While the rice is cooking, toast the saffron strands in a small pan over very low heat for 1 to 2 minutes. When cooled, crush them and combine them with 1 tablespoon of warm water in a small bowl.

Remove 1 cup of the cooked rice and combine it with the saffron mixture. Stir well so that the rice turns yellow.

Preheat the oven to 250ºF and use two 9 x 13-inch baking pans: Beginning with the first pan, spread one quarter of the white rice on the bottom, top with one quarter of the meat mixture, another layer of one quarter of the white rice, and another layer of one quarter of the meat mixture. Sprinkle with half of the cashews and half of the raisins, if desired. Sprinkle half of the yellow saffron rice on top to add color. Repeat this process with the remaining pan.

Cover with foil and bake for 20 to 25 minutes. Top the rice with the reserved fried onions, egg slices, if desired, and cilantro before serving.

Cashew Nut Chicken

Kaju Murghi

Makes 6 servings

This chicken curry is infused with the flavor of cashews. My mother recommends buying unroasted nuts for this recipe and roasting them yourself. Place them on a tray in a 350°F oven for about ten minutes. The fresh roasted taste is really worth this extra step. You can also substitute other chicken parts for boneless, skinless breasts; just be sure to remove the skin and any excess fat. Serve with hot rice or flatbreads.

---

2 tablespoons oil

3 medium onions, finely chopped

2 tablespoons garlic-ginger paste

3 medium-size tomatoes, chopped

1 teaspoon ground cayenne pepper

1 teaspoon whole cumin seeds, crushed

1 teaspoon salt

3 pounds boneless, skinless chicken breasts, cut into bite-size pieces

1 teaspoon sugar

$^1/_2$ cup cashew nuts, lightly toasted

 Heat the oil in a large pot over medium-low heat. Add the onions and sauté until golden brown, about 5 to 10 minutes. Add the garlic-ginger paste and sauté for 1 to 2 minutes. Add the tomatoes and sauté for 5 minutes, until a sauce forms and thickens.

Add the cayenne pepper, cumin seeds, and salt. Sauté for 2 minutes to release the flavors of the spices. Add the chicken and mix well to coat with the spices and brown, about 5 minutes. Add $1^1/_2$ cups of water, reduce the heat to low, cover and cook until the chicken is tender, about 20 minutes.

Add the sugar and cashew nuts, stir, and cook for 10 minutes more until the chicken is completely done and the sauce is thickened. Add a few tablespoons of water if the sauce is too thick.

Egg Curry

Inda ni curry

Makes 6 servings

For nonvegetarians and vegetarians who eat eggs, this is a hearty, delicious curry. It is particularly good served over shredded chapati, but works well with rice too.

---

2 tablespoons oil

1 large onion, finely chopped

3 tablespoons garlic-ginger paste

1 teaspoon ground cayenne pepper

1 teaspoon turmeric

1 teaspoon ground cumin

1 teaspoon ground coriander

$^1/_2$ to 1 teaspoon *garam masala*, to taste

2 medium-size tomatoes, diced

3 small potatoes, boiled, peeled, and chopped

6 eggs, hard-boiled and peeled

$^1/_4$ cup chopped fresh cilantro

2 tablespoons chopped mint

Heat the oil in a medium-size pot over medium heat. Add the onions and sauté for 5 to 7 minutes, until the onions are browned. Add the garlic-ginger paste, cayenne, turmeric, cumin, coriander, and *garam masala*. Stir well and cook for 1 to 2 minutes to release the flavors of the spices.

Reduce the heat to low and add the tomatoes. Cook for about 5 minutes, until a sauce forms. Add the potatoes and $1^1/_2$ to 2 cups of water, depending on the desired thickness of the curry. Stir well.

Make a 1-inch incision along the length of each egg so the curry can flavor the eggs throughout and add the eggs to the curry. Cover, and cook for 10 minutes, stirring occasionally. Garnish with cilantro and mint before serving.

Shrimp Curry

Jhinga ni curry

This zesty shrimp curry gets its kick from the combination of spices and lime juice, and its heartiness from the potatoes. It is delicious served over plain basmati rice or with flatbreads.

---

3 tablespoons oil

1 medium onion, chopped

$1/2$ medium green bell pepper, chopped

4 teaspoons garlic-ginger paste

1 teaspoon ground cayenne pepper

1 teaspoon turmeric

$1^1/2$ teaspoons ground coriander

$1/2$ teaspoon ground cumin

$3/4$ teaspoon salt

1 teaspoon *garam masala*

2 medium-size potatoes, peeled and cut into bite-size chunks

1 pound large shrimp, peeled and deveined

Juice of $1/2$ lime

$1/4$ cup chopped fresh cilantro

 Heat the oil in medium-size pot over medium heat. Add the onion and sauté for 5 to 10 minutes, until soft. Add the bell peppers and continue to sauté for about 5 minutes.

Add the garlic-ginger paste and stir well. Reduce the heat to medium-low, and continue to cook, stirring frequently to avoid sticking, for 5 minutes, until the onions are brown.

Add the cayenne, turmeric, coriander, cumin, salt and *garam masala*. Stir well. Add the potatoes and $1^1/2$ cups of water. Cover and cook for 10 to 15 minutes, until the potatoes are cooked, stirring occasionally.

Add the shrimp and cook for 2 to 3 minutes, until cooked through. Stir in the lime juice and sprinkle with cilantro before serving.

Spicy Shrimp and Tomatoes

Masala Jhinga

Makes 4 servings

Here is another shrimp recipe that makes a moist, tangy dish without a sauce or curry. This version is nice served over plain rice but is especially good with *Chapatis* (page 49) or Puris (page 50).

1 pound shrimp, peeled and deveined	$^1/_2$ teaspoon ground cumin
2 tablespoons oil	$^1/_2$ teaspoon ground coriander
2 medium onions, chopped fine	1 teaspoon salt
2 tablespoons garlic-ginger paste	1 medium-size tomato, chopped
$^1/_2$ teaspoon ground cayenne pepper	2 tablespoons chopped fresh cilantro
$^1/_2$ teaspoon turmeric	

 Wash the shrimp in a bowl of salted water. Drain and set aside.

Heat the oil in a medium-size skillet over medium-low heat. Add the onions and sauté until softened, about 3 to 5 minutes. Add the garlic-ginger paste, cayenne pepper, turmeric, cumin, coriander, and salt. Stir well and sauté for 1 minute.

Add the shrimp. Stir and cook for 3 to 5 minutes, until the shrimp turn pink. Add the tomatoes and continue to cook for 2 to 3 minutes. Garnish with cilantro before serving.

Masala-Coated Fish Fillets

Masala Machi   Makes 4 to 6 servings

A good variety of fish is available in Gujarat, particularly in coastal areas but also near rivers and lakes. Any mild, white-fleshed fish will work for this recipe. Some suggestions are catfish, cod, flounder, halibut, or sole. This spicy dish is excellent served with hot basmati rice and vegetables. Remember to allow time for the fish to marinate.

3 pounds (4 to 6) fish fillets (such as catfish, cod, or flounder)	1 teaspoon ground cayenne pepper
1/2 teaspoon salt	1 teaspoon ground cumin
Juice of 1 lemon	1 teaspoon ground coriander
1 tablespoon garlic-ginger paste	1 teaspoon garam masala
	2 to 3 tablespoons oil

 Sprinkle the fish with salt and lemon juice. Cover with plastic wrap and set aside in the refrigerator for 30 minutes.

In the meantime, combine the garlic-ginger paste, cayenne, cumin, coriander, and garam masala in a small bowl.

Remove the fish from the refrigerator and coat each fillet with the spice mixture. Cover and marinate in the refrigerator for 1 hour.

Heat the oil in a skillet or frying pan over medium heat. Add the fish and cook for 3 to 4 minutes on each side, or until cooked through. Use a spatula to turn the fillets very carefully to avoid breaking them.

Fish in Banana Leaves

Patra ni Machi

Makes 6 servings

This is the Parsi method of cooking fish. The fish fillets are coated with tasty chutney and then wrapped in banana leaves to cook. Banana leaves are sometimes available frozen at Indian grocery stores. If you cannot find them, substitute foil.

3 large banana leaves or 6 pieces of aluminum foil	1 recipe Cilantro Chutney (see page 118)
6 fish fillets (3 pounds) such as cod, flounder, halibut, or catfish	1/2 cup white vinegar

 Remove the center stem from the banana leaves so that you have six pieces. Place one fish fillet on each banana leaf and coat it with the chutney. Wrap each banana leaf around the fish and tie with oven-safe cooking string. Alternatively, place the fish on a piece of foil, coat with the chutney, sprinkle with 1 to 2 tablespoons of water, and seal into a package with the second piece of foil.

Heat the oven to 350°F. Place the fish packets on a tray. If using banana leaves, grease the tray with oil first, and sprinkle 1/2 cup of water and 1/2 cup of vinegar on top of the leaves. If using foil, proceed directly with baking the fish. Bake for 10 minutes, then turn over and bake for an additional 10 minutes, or until the fish is cooked. Serve with rice.

Chutneys, Pickles, and Condiments

Raita

Matto

Makes 1 1/2 cups

This creamy yogurt sauce is an enticing accompaniment to spicy meat and vegetable dishes, particularly Biryani (page 106) and Chicken Curry (page 101). The coolness of the yogurt and cucumber cuts the fire of chilies and other spices. Frying the mustard seeds and curry leaves in ghee before they are combined with the yogurt releases their strong flavors. This is a favorite dish served alongside Biryani at our house during winter holidays, when pomegranates are in season. We love to include pomegranate seeds for their beautiful color and tart refreshing flavor. In summer, seasonal tomatoes make an equally delicious addition.

---

1 cup plain yogurt

1 teaspoon ghee

1/2 teaspoon black mustard seeds

10 to 12 dried curry leaves

1/2 teaspoon whole cumin seeds, or 1/4 teaspoon ground cumin

1/2 medium cucumber, peeled and grated

1/4 cup chopped fresh cilantro

1 small or plum tomato, chopped (optional)

1/2 cup pomegranate seeds (optional)

 Whisk the yogurt with 1/4 cup water until smooth.

Heat the ghee in a small skillet over medium heat and add the mustard seeds. When they begin to pop, add the curry leaves. Turn off the heat and let the mixture rest for 1 minute. Slowly and carefully pour the ghee mixture into the yogurt and immediately whisk together.

To make freshly ground cumin, heat the oven to 350ºF. Place the cumin seeds on a tray and roast them in oven for 5 to 10 minutes. Remove the seeds from the oven, place in blender or spice grinder, and grind to a fine powder.

Add the ground cumin, cucumber, cilantro, and tomato or pomegranate seeds to the yogurt mixture. Stir well before serving.

Cilantro Chutney

Kothmir ni chutney

This chutney is easy to prepare and can be served with virtually any dish. Store leftovers in the refrigerator in an airtight container for up to one week.

---

1 bunch cilantro, washed and stemmed
1¹/2 teaspoons garlic-ginger paste
1 green chili pepper, stem removed
¹/4 cup raw peanuts
¹/4 teaspoon ground cumin
¹/2 teaspoon salt

¹/2 teaspoon sugar
1 teaspoon lemon juice
¹/2 medium-size tomato, quartered
   (optional)
2 tablespoons mint leaves (optional)

 Combine all the ingredients in a blender and process until smooth, adding 1 to 2 tablespoons water if necessary.

Tamarind Chutney

Makes $1/4$ to $1/2$ cup of chutney

Tamarind Chutney is generally sweet but can be made spicier with the addition of more red pepper or minced green chili. Leftovers can be stored in an airtight container in the refrigerator for one to two weeks.

---

2 tablespoons tamarind paste
$1/4$ teaspoon ground cayenne pepper
$1/4$ teaspoon salt
1 teaspoon brown sugar

Optional ingredients:

1 tablespoon finely chopped golden raisins
1 date, finely chopped
$1/2$ to 1 green chili, stemmed and minced
2 tablespoons finely chopped fresh cilantro

 Combine all the ingredients, including any desired optional ingredients with 1 tablespoon water. Mix well. Add 1 to 2 tablespoons additional water for a more liquid chutney.

Fenugreek-Infused Mango Pickle

Methia Keri Athanu   Makes 64 ounces

Though this is a spicy pickle, the sweet hints of mango come through. Use green or unripe mangoes because they have a nice tart flavor and will not fall apart like ripe mangoes, which are too soft and juicy for this recipe. A teaspoon or two of this pickle is eaten as a condiment alongside rice and dal or vegetables. Be sure to wash your hands carefully and keep all utensils and jars very clean to prevent bacteria from contaminating the pickles. This recipe takes a few days, but your patience will be rewarded!

---

5 pounds (about 4 to 5) green (unripe)
   mangoes
1 cup salt
3 cups oil
1 cup fenugreek seeds, crushed

$1/4$ to $1/2$ cup ground cayenne pepper
1 teaspoon turmeric
1 teaspoon asafoetida powder

Wash the mangoes thoroughly and cut them into 2-inch chunks (do not peel them). Place the mango pieces in a bowl and sprinkle with 2 to 3 tablespoons of the salt. Mix well with a clean spoon. Cover and set aside at room temperature for 24 hours.

Drain any liquid from the mango pieces and spread them on a tray lined with a clean cloth or paper towels. Allow the pieces to dry at room temperature for at least 12 hours. Avoid touching them to keep bacteria away.

Heat 2 cups of the oil in a pan over medium heat. Add the fenugreek seeds, and stir for 1 to 2 minutes, until they are lightly browned. Reduce the heat to medium-low, add the cayenne, turmeric, asafoetida powder, and the remaining salt. Stir and cook for 2 to 3 minutes. Remove from the heat and set aside to cool.

In a large bowl, combine the mango pieces and the oil mixture. Use a spoon to stir very well until all the mango pieces are well coated. Pour the mixture into one sterilized 64-ounce jar or two 32-ounce jars. Seal the jar(s) and set aside at room temperature for 24 hours.

Heat the remaining 1 cup of oil to release its flavors. Cool the oil and then pour it into the jar(s). Make sure all the mango pieces are submerged in the oil. Close the jar(s) and set aside for 2 days at room temperature. After that, the pickle is ready to eat.

Note: The pickle will keep for up to six months in a cool, dry cabinet. Be sure to handle it with a clean spoon every time.

Lime Pickle

Limbu nu athanu (achar)

This pickle features the tart flavor of limes combined with the sweetness of *gur* (Indian brown sugar, see page 18). It can be enjoyed alongside any meal. It will take about two and a half weeks to prepare.

---

10 to 12 limes	8 teaspoons fenugreek seeds, lightly crushed
2 tablespoons salt	1 teaspoon ground cayenne pepper
1 teaspoon turmeric	1 cup *gur*
2 tablespoons oil	

 Wash the limes thoroughly and quarter them, *being careful not to slice all the way through* so that they are left intact at the bottom. Combine the limes, salt, and turmeric in a bowl and mix thoroughly. Pour this mixture into a sterilized 40-ounce jar, close it, and set aside in a cool, dry place for 2 weeks.

Spread the limes on a tray lined with a clean cloth or paper towels. Set aside and dry on a countertop for 2 days. Avoid touching the limes so that they do not develop any bacteria.

Separate the lime quarters and then cut each quarter in half so that each lime produces eight pieces.

Heat the oil in a large pot over medium heat. Add the fenugreek seeds and sauté for 1 minute, until the seeds are browned. Reduce the heat to low, add the cayenne and *gur*, stirring well. Stir and cook for 2 to 3 minutes, until the *gur* melts and a sauce is formed. Cool completely.

Add the lime pieces to the gur mixture. Stir to coat thoroughly. Pour the mixture into a sterilized 40-ounce jar. Set aside at room temperature for 2 days, after which the pickle will be ready to eat. Once opened, it is safer to refrigerate them.

Note: Always use clean utensils to handle the pickle and close the lid tightly again to avoid introducing bacteria.

Sweets and Beverages

Rich Ricotta Squares

Barfi

Makes 12 to 15 squares

Because most Indian kitchens lack ovens, you will not find many baked desserts. Instead, treats like *Barfi*, made on the stovetop, are popular.

---

³/₄ cup sugar

1 (15-ounce) container whole-milk ricotta cheese

3 tablespoons butter or ghee

¹/₄ cup powdered milk

For garnish:

almond slices

crushed pistachios

ground cardamom

In a small pan, combine the sugar with ¹/₄ cup of water over low heat, stirring constantly until it forms a syrup, about 2 to 3 minutes. Set aside.

In a separate pan, heat the ricotta over very low heat. Add the butter, stirring constantly until the liquid evaporates and the mixture thickens, about 10 to 15 minutes. Add the sugar syrup and powdered milk, and continue to cook and stir over very low heat for 2 to 3 minutes.

Spread the mixture into a greased 9 x 13-inch pan. Sprinkle with desired garnishes. When cooled, cut into squares and serve.

Date Slices

Makes about 20 slices

Here is another popular dessert that makes use of pantry ingredients and does not require any baking.

1¹/₂ to 2 cups dates	1 teaspoon ground cardamom
¹/₂ cup whole milk	¹/₄ cup chopped almonds
2 cups powdered milk	
1 (14-ounce) can sweetened condensed milk	

 Cut the dates into very small pieces and soak in the milk for 1 to 2 hours. Place the date mixture in a blender and process until smooth.

Combine the date mixture with the powdered milk, condensed milk, and cardamom in a pan over medium heat. Stir frequently until the mixture forms a dough, about 10 to 15 minutes. Remove from heat. Alternatively, combine the ingredients in a microwave-safe dish and microwave on HIGH for 5 minutes, stirring midway, until it achieves the texture of dough. Microwave for an additional 1 to 2 minutes if necessary.

When the dough is cool enough to work with, form it into a long, sausagelike roll. Cover with plastic wrap and refrigerate for 6 hours.

To serve, cut slices from the roll and top with almond pieces.

Sweet Condensed Milk Balls

Penda

These creamy milk balls are available in different varieties in sweetshops all over Gujarat. Many Indian groceries now also carry traditional sweets, but these are easy to make at home.

1 stick (8 tablespoons) butter or margarine	For garnish:
1 (14-ounce) can sweetened condensed milk	crushed almonds
1 cup powdered milk	crushed pistachios

In a medium-size pan, melt the butter over low heat. Add the condensed milk and stir until the mixture thickens, about 5 to 7 minutes. Reduce the heat to very low, add the powdered milk and continue to cook and stir for 5 minutes, then remove from the heat.

When cooled, take about 1 tablespoon of the mixture at a time, and form into 10 to 12 small balls. Make a depression into the center of each ball with your finger and sprinkle with the desired garnish.

Sweet Dough Balls with Coconut

Coconut Gulab Jamun

Makes 10 to 12 balls

Gulab jamun are a classic Indian dessert, usually served in a thick, sweet syrup. Here is an alternative that is rolled in coconut instead.

---

2 cups all-purpose flour
1 tablespoon ground cardamom
1 teaspoon ground nutmeg
1 teaspoon baking soda

1 (14-ounce) can sweetened condensed milk
1 cup oil
1/2 cup unsweetened flaked coconut

In a medium-size bowl, combine the flour, cardamom, nutmeg, and baking soda.

In a small pan over low heat, heat the condensed milk until it is warmed through.

Slowly add the condensed milk to the flour mixture, stirring constantly. When the mixture has cooled slightly, lightly oil your hands and knead it into a soft dough. Form the dough into 10 to 12 small, egg-shaped balls about 1 1/2 inches in diameter.

Heat the oil in a deep pan or *kadhai* over low heat and deep-fry the balls until golden brown, about 1 to 2 minutes.

Drain the balls on paper towels to remove excess oil. When slightly cooled, roll them in coconut and serve.

Bottle Gourd Halwa

Doodhi no halwo

Makes 40 squares

This sweet treat, a rich indulgence made with an entire pound of butter, is perfect for a party or crowd. Bottle gourds are readily available at Indian grocery stores. Their tender, slightly sweet flesh is perfect for desserts such as this *halwa*. Culinary rose essence, also known as rose water, is available at Indian groceries.

1 pound bottle gourd *(doodhi)*	1 pound (4 sticks) butter
1 tablespoon ghee	$2^1/4$ cups sugar
20 almonds	3 cups powdered milk
20 cashews	$1/2$ teaspoon rose essence or vanilla extract
20 pistachios	
1 (15-ounce) container whole-milk ricotta cheese	4 to 5 drops green food coloring

 Grease a 9 x 13-inch pan.

Peel and grate the bottle gourd. Heat the ghee in a medium-size pan over medium-low heat. Add the grated gourd and sauté for 5 to 7 minutes, until most of the moisture evaporates. Set aside to cool.

Chop the almonds, cashews, and pistachios into small pieces and combine. Set aside.

In a large pot, combine the ricotta cheese and butter over low heat. Cook for 5 minutes, until the butter is melted. Add the sugar, stirring constantly so that it does not stick to the bottom of the pot. Add the gourd and stir thoroughly. Add the powdered milk, a little at a time, stirring continuously. Add half the chopped nuts, and all of the rose essence and the food coloring. Stir for 1 to 2 minutes, until the ingredients are thoroughly combined and the mixture turns green. Remove from the heat.

Spread the mixture into the prepared pan. Use a spatula to spread it evenly and flatten it. The mixture should be about 1 to $1^1/2$ inches thick. Top with the remaining nut mixture and cut into about forty small squares.

Sweet Yogurt Dessert

Shrikhand

Makes 4 to 6 servings

Shrikhand is a typical sweet served in Gujarat and throughout India. Its name translates to "ambrosia of the gods." Made with rich, creamy yogurt, precious saffron, delicate cardamom, and fragrant rose essence, it certainly lives up to this claim! For variety, you can also top *shrikhand* with canned mixed fruits, chopped pineapple, strawberries or mango. Serve with Puris (see page 50).

---

4 cups plain whole-milk yogurt
$^1/_2$ teaspoon saffron strands
1 tablespoon milk, warm
1 cup sugar
1$^1/_2$ teaspoons ground cardamom

$^1/_2$ teaspoon rose essence or vanilla extract
1 tablespoon chopped almonds
1 tablespoon chopped pistachios

 Place the yogurt in cheesecloth over a bowl for 3 hours to drain excess water.

Meanwhile, combine the saffron with the milk and soak for 1 to 2 hours.

Mix the yogurt, saffron mixture, sugar, cardamom, and rose essence well with an electric mixer. Cover with plastic wrap and refrigerate for at least 3 hours.

Top with almonds and pistachios before serving.

Sweet Porridge

Sheero

Makes 8 to 10 servings

Rich in ghee and sugar, this porridge is an indulgent treat. It is wonderful served warm for breakfast or an afternoon snack. This sweet is also served to new mothers to help them regain their strength.

$3/4$ cup ghee or butter ($1^1/2$ sticks)	1 teaspoon ground cardamom
2 cups uncooked Cream of Wheat	2 tablespoons raisins
2 cups whole milk	1 tablespoon chopped almonds,
$^1/2$ to 1 cup sugar, according to taste	pistachios, or other nuts

Melt the ghee in a large nonstick pan over medium-low heat. Add the Cream of Wheat and sauté until golden brown. Add the milk, sugar, and cardamom, and continue to stir as the mixture thickens. Add the raisins and stir well.

Continue to cook, stirring, for about 5 to 10 minutes, until the porridge thickens and the ghee starts to separate from it. Remove from the heat and stir in the nuts. Serve warm.

Coconut-Filled Pastries

Ghoogra

Makes 16 pastries

These pastries are a favorite around our house during the winter holidays. They keep for several days when stored in an airtight container, so are always handy for a snack or breakfast treat.

For the stuffing:

$^1/_4$ cup uncooked Cream of Wheat

$^1/_4$ cup grated sweetened coconut

1 tablespoon ghee

2 teaspoons poppy seeds

1 teaspoon ground cinnamon

1 teaspoon ground cloves

1 teaspoon ground cardamom

1 cup sugar

For the dough:

2 cups chapati flour

1 teaspoon salt

$^1/_2$ teaspoon turmeric

$^1/_4$ cup oil

$1^1/_2$ cups oil for deep-frying

 To prepare the filling, combine the Cream of Wheat, coconut, ghee, poppy seeds, cinnamon, cloves, and cardamom in a medium-size pan over low heat. Stir until the mixture turns light brown. Remove from the heat and stir in the sugar.

To prepare the dough, combine the flour, salt, turmeric, and oil in a medium-size bowl. Mix well with your hands. Slowly add $^1/_4$ cup of warm water, a few tablespoons at a time, and knead into firm dough.

Divide the dough into sixteen small balls. Roll each ball into a circle about 3 inches in diameter. Place $1^1/_2$ teaspoons of coconut filling on the top half and bring the bottom half of the circle up to form a semicircle. Moisten the edges with a few drops of water and seal. You can also press them together with the tines of a fork to reinforce the seal and make a nice design. Repeat this process for the remaining dough and stuffing.

Heat the $1^1/_2$ cups of oil in a deep pan or *kadhai* over medium-low heat. Fry the pastries, two or three at a time, for 1 to 2 minutes, turning midway, until golden brown. Drain on a plate lined with paper towels.

Sugary Wheat Balls

Ladva

These sugary balls are a typical winter holiday treat around our house. I have fond memories of my aunts sitting together in the kitchen, chatting and laughing while they rolled the balls.

1 1/2 cups uncooked Cream of Wheat	2 tablespoons ground cardamom
1/2 cup chapati flour	1/2 cup crushed almonds
1 3/4 cups butter or ghee	1/4 cup pistachios
2 cups oil for deep-frying	1 cup raisins
1 cup sugar	

Combine the Cream of Wheat, chapati flour, and 3/4 cup of the ghee in a medium-size bowl. Mix well. Slowly add 1/4 cup of warm water and knead into a firm dough. Take a ball of dough, about 2 1/2 inches in diameter, in your palm and flatten it into an oval patty. Repeat with the remaining dough.

Heat the oil in a deep pan or *kadhai* over medium heat. Deep-fry the dough, a few pieces at a time, for 2 to 3 minutes, until golden brown. Drain on paper towels.

Break the fried dough into pieces and place them in a blender or food processor while still warm. Process until they resemble fine meal. Sift through a sieve and collect in a large bowl. Put any hard pieces through the blender again.

Warm the remaining ghee. Make a well in the meal mixture and pour in the ghee. Mix well with your hands. Add the sugar, cardamom, almonds, pistachios, and raisins to the meal mixture. Mix well. Warm the mixture slightly, either by microwaving it for 15 seconds or so or heating it over low heat on the stove for 1 to 2 minutes. This will help to combine the ingredients and make the mixture softer and easier to work with. Take a 2-inch chunk of the mixture and press it together hard to make a firm, dense ball about the size of a golf ball. Repeat with the remaining mixture. Let the balls set for 30 minutes in refrigerator, or 3 to 4 hours on a countertop, before serving.

Mango Frozen Yogurt

Makes 4 to 6 servings

This is my solution to cravings for mango ice cream. Made with wholesome yogurt, this recipe is much lower in fat and much easier to prepare. You can use vanilla-flavored yogurt, but I've found that plain works just as well because the mango pulp is so sweet. Mango pulp is readily available in Indian grocery stores. You can also add diced mango if desired. It is best served as soon as you make it.

3 cups vanilla or plain low-fat yogurt	1 teaspoon ground cardamom
1 cup mango pulp	

 Combine the ingredients in a large pitcher or bowl. Stir thoroughly.

Pour the mixture into an ice-cream maker and follow the manufacturer's directions.

Cardamom-Flavored Milk

Makes 1 serving

This flavorful hot milk drink can be enjoyed at breakfast or any time of the day!

1^1/$_2$ cups milk, heated	Pinch of saffron
^{1}/$_4$ teaspoon ground cardamom	

 Combine the ingredients and stir. Serve hot.

Almond-Pistachio-Flavored Milk

Makes 1 serving

A glass of this fragrant milk is the perfect way to begin or end the day.

3 almonds	¹/₄ teaspoon ground cardamom
2 pistachios	Pinch of saffron
1¹/₂ cups hot milk	

 Soak the almonds and pistachios in warm water for 30 minutes. Remove the skins. Crush the nuts with a mortar and pestle, or process in a blender.

Combine the nut mixture with the remaining ingredients and stir well. Serve hot.

Simple Tea

Chai

Makes 4 servings

Indians are avid tea drinkers and you will find many varieties of tea available at Indian groceries. Loose tea provides the most robust flavor, but you can substitute tea bags in these recipes as well.

1 tablespoon loose black tea leaves	Sugar
1 cup milk, heated	

 In a small pan, bring 3 cups of water to a boil. Add the tea leaves and soak to desired flavor, 2 to 5 minutes. Add the hot milk and bring to a boil again.

Strain the tea into four cups. Add sugar to taste before serving.

Masala Tea

Masala Chai

This is tea with the works! It can be enjoyed as an everyday indulgence or reserved for special occasions. Either way, it should be sipped slowly to savor the flavors.

2 stalks lemongrass	1 cup milk, heated
½-inch piece fresh ginger, peeled	sugar
1 tablespoon black tea leaves	

 In a small pan, bring 3 cups of water to a boil. Add the lemongrass and ginger. Add the tea and soak to desired flavor, 2 to 5 minutes. Add the hot milk and return to a boil.

Strain the tea into four cups. Add sugar as desired before serving.

Suggested Menus

Vegetarian Lunch
Eggplant, Potato and Tomato Curry (page 76)
Gujarati Dal (page 92)
Plain Basmati Rice (page 57)
Chapatis (page 49)
Lime Pickle (page 122)

A Traditional Gujarati *Thaali* Vegetarian Dinner
You can purchase traditional Indian *thaalis* (stainless steel plates) along with little insert cups at most Indian grocery stores. Serve each dish in a separate cup and then arrange them all, along with a mound of rice and some hot puris, in the larger *thaali*.

Spicy Dumplings in Yogurt Sauce (page 32)
Okra with Potatoes (page 69)
Classic Gujarati Mixed Vegetables (page 66)
Gujarati Yogurt Curry (page 93)
Seasoned Rice with Lentils (page 60)
Shobha Foi's Puris (page 50)
Fenugreek-Infused Mango Pickle (page 120)
Sweet Yogurt Dessert (Shrikhand) (page 130)

A Nonvegetarian Feast
Cocktail-Size Meat Samosas (page 46)
Cabbage, Potatoes and Pigeon Peas (page 84)
Chicken Biryani (page 106)
Raita (page 117)
Chapatis (page 49)
Sweet Porridge (page 131)

Index